GOD CARES ENOUGH

THE MESSAGE OF JONAH

L. Edward Hazelbaker
with David L. Raines

GOD CARES ENOUGH

THE MESSAGE OF JONAH

L. Edward Hazelbaker
with David L. Raines

BRIDGE LOGOS

Newberry, FL 32669

Bridge-Logos
Newberry, FL 32669

God Cares Enough: The Message of Jonah

Printed in the United States of America.

Library of Congress Catalog Card Number: 2023949494

International Standard Book Number: 978-1-61036-996-1

The Author's Website: TheWornKeyboard.com
The Author's E-mail: L.Edward@TheWornKeyboard.com

Interior Layout and Cover Design: Ashley Morgan
GraphicGardenLLC@gmail.com

BP 02/2024

WHAT OTHERS ARE SAYING

It's not easy to preach or write about famous Bible characters—especially the runaway prophet, Jonah. However, in *God Cares Enough: The Message of Jonah,* L. Edward has made a great contribution to the story of this unique man who was called of God but ran from the Lord and the assignment he received. Through all the twists and turns of Jonah's desires and actions to avoid what he was called to do, Hazelbaker provides us with a powerful teaching on the depths of God's care, not just for Jonah but for all of us. I was challenged by this book. The way the author unfolds Jonah's journey is inspiring and provides instruction for us in such a way that the Lord's care comes alive and makes it applicable to all believers—regardless of their ages and stages in their spiritual journey. God cared enough to stick with Jonah, as He does for all of His children, and that care is so powerfully told in this book that I am honored to share my endorsement.

—**Rev. Don Wilkerson,** Co-founder,
Teen Challenge and Times Square Church
President Emeritus, Teen Challenge, Inc.

I have served as a prison chaplain at the highest security prisons of the land. The men and women of those prisons are the most vile and violent people you can encounter. The atrocities they committed can cause anyone to call for their destruction. I have heard many people, including those in churches, ask me why I bothered with them. They say things like, "Put them in jail and throw away the key. Let them rot there on their way to hell." However, God cares enough to offer grace; and *God Cares Enough: The Message of Jonah,* has reminded me of that. I recommend you read this book with an open mind and receptive spirit. L. Edward Hazelbaker is going to gently challenge you through it to consider the depth of God's Grace. God cares more than you can ever think!

—**Rev. Manuel A. Cordero,** Senior Director
Assemblies of God Chaplaincy Ministries

When I consider the moments of greatest challenge in my faith journey, a common denominator at those times has been my lack of meditation on the character of God, namely His compassion. L. Edward Hazelbaker's captivating, easy-to-read, practical, and impactful book on the story of Jonah has reminded me again of the critical need to contemplate how the compassion of Father God enables me to see myself and others as He does. I recommend you read *God Cares Enough: The Message of Jonah,* because really knowing that God cares enough—as Lynn insightfully describes in chapter after chapter—actually has the potential of moving us into action with Him. And this world sorely needs individuals who know and live out the nature of our compassionate God. Get ready to be truly inspired and challenged as you read and become profoundly reminded that God certainly does care enough!

—**Rev. Darren Pilcher,** Executive Presbyter
Oklahoma Assemblies of God

DEDICATION

I dedicate this book to the memory of Reverend David L. Raines, my friend, spiritual mentor, and pastor for eighteen years, and to his wife, Bertha. More than anyone else, the two of them instilled within me a love for the truth of God's Word and the obligation to allow the words of the Bible themselves to have preeminence in not only influencing but also forming my beliefs as a Christian.

My wife, Melveta, and I, and David and Bertha, raised our families in the same town and church, and I was privileged to serve as David's associate. Our families spent a lot of time together, and we became close—as much like family as we could be without being related.

This book was birthed from a series of sermons David developed and delivered during his tenure as pastor of Perkins Assembly of God in Perkins, Oklahoma. That series of sermons was the result of much preparation and prayer on David's part. And it had a great impact on me.

Several years after he delivered the sermon series, I offered to co-author a book with him using his sermons on the book of Jonah as the inspiration. I eventually started that work, and over time I developed and completed the first draft of a manuscript using the sermon notes he provided to me and my own memory of the sermons as the work's foundation. But by then, his health had failed to the point that he was not able to collaborate in it further.

David didn't get through a review of the first draft of the manuscript because of his health, and we never discussed it again. I then allowed the draft to languish from 2017 to 2023 —two years after he moved to heaven—when I decided to start working on it again.

After once again taking up the work, I continued to enlarge the manuscript in my attempt to increase the book's value and expand on its theme. There are now additional points and many of my own thoughts in the book that I developed without David's input, but the theme and points expressed in his sermons are what formed the foundation upon which this book was built.

Without Pastor Raines having preached his series on *God Cares Enough* many years ago, I likely would not have been able to develop my current understanding of the story of Jonah and fully grasp the significance of what I now relate to you in this book.

—LEH

FOREWORD

L. Edward Hazelbaker is an inspiring author, teacher, and pastor. In his latest book, *God Cares Enough,* the reader is guided through a masterful study of the book of Jonah. Each chapter reveals another aspect of the caring nature of our Heavenly Father. Lynn unfolds the timely truth that while most of us, like Jonah, are interested in getting rid of problems, "God is more interested in fixing them." This study challenges the reader to develop a supernatural sense of God's care within our own hearts. I know this book will inspire you. I highly recommend *God Cares Enough: The Message of Jonah.*

—**Dr. D. E. Wootton,** Superintendent
Oklahoma Assemblies of God

TABLE OF CONTENTS

GOD CARES ENOUGH

INTRODUCTION

Does God care? The answer is an emphatic, "Yes!"

The answer seems apparent for anyone who has a concept of what God did to provide us with a path to redemption. After all, the Bible reveals that He cared enough for us to offer up as a sacrifice *"his one and only Son, so that everyone who believes in him will not perish but have eternal life"* (John 3:16b).

"Jesus died on the cross to pay for our sins. Of course God cares! Why ask?"

The reason I'm asking becomes clearer as we start answering that question by closely examining the events contained in the Book of Jonah. For by delving thoughtfully and deeply into the story of Jonah in this book, we'll see the truth and extent of our Lord's care.

If you have ever questioned God's interests and concern for the world, I hope by reading this book you'll soon come to understand and accept the vastness of His concern for both you and others. And after completing our study and coming to grips with the entire message the Lord gave to us in the Book of Jonah, I trust you will never again question His care.

This book examines important truths that God revealed through Jonah's experiences, and the Lord wants us to learn them well. Hopefully, after reading this book you'll better understand, value, and accept all of those truths as you gain a new appreciation of God's care for us and the world around us—for everyone.

Sometimes it seems the Book of Jonah is largely relegated to a story told to children, with a single, easy-to-understand message they'll be able to grasp. But it has much more to say than what the majority of people probably think. Through a more detailed handling of the short Book of Jonah, we'll find that Jonah's experiences and the actions of the Lord recorded in the thirty-second book of the Old Testament go far beyond delivering to us a simple one-faceted *moral of the story.*

The Book of Jonah reveals to us that God cares, yes; but beyond that, the account of His dealings with both Jonah and Nineveh goes much deeper. The story of Jonah goes beyond answering the question, "Does God care?" It answers the more challenging question of, "How *much* does God care?"

The extent of His care for the lost, wicked populace of Nineveh is the backdrop for the theme of how much God cares. However, the story of Jonah doesn't just reveal the level of God's care for the evil city of Nineveh. It moves on to reveal to us the degree to which He cares for much more—including His own followers, even when they're being disobedient in their actions toward Him.

But there's even more to learn.

Should God care? Should He be concerned? In case anyone thinks such questions silly or not worth posing, let's come to understand that the Lord, himself, thought such a question worth asking.

The Book of Jonah is unique in the Bible for the way it ends. It ends with God asking Jonah the same basic question, and no response to the question from Jonah is recorded. But the question God asked was not simply rhetorical. It was a valid question that He pressed upon Jonah to not just consider but decide how to answer.

It was an extremely important question. And by the time we close this study of the Book of Jonah, we'll understand that through the events played out in that chapter in Jonah's life, God was proving and providing to Jonah the answer He expected to hear from him.

As the world's preeminent teacher, by using circumstances and events that challenged Jonah's understanding and personal beliefs to the very core of his existence, the Holy Spirit was without doubt particularly active in teaching and revealing to Jonah the true measure of God's care. The question had to be asked, and like any other student, Jonah's answer would show if he learned what his teacher was teaching him.

But since Jonah's story is included in the Bible, it's clear that God's intention has always been for the Holy Spirit's lessons contained within it to be delivered to more than the mind and heart of only one stubborn man. The Lord also wants us—you and me—to understand the depth of His care. Hopefully God will have an easier time teaching us about it, and we'll more readily receive and learn the lessons!

Hopefully we'll yield ourselves to the Holy Spirit's efforts to enlighten us without having to experience so much spiritual distress and physical trauma as that suffered by Jonah. But truly, our own interests in learning, and our willingness to give the Lord the response He's looking for, is up to us.

How much does God care? Does He care enough? He will answer those questions for us as we study the Book of Jonah.

—L. Edward

CHAPTER 1

GOD CARES ENOUGH TO CALL A PREACHER

The L*ORD* *gave this message to Jonah son of Amittai: "Get up and go to the great city of Nineveh. Announce my judgment against it because I have seen how wicked its people are."*

(Jonah 1:1–2)

THE NARRATIVE CONTAINED in the book of Jonah begins abruptly. The writer spends no time setting the scene. He provides no details about Jonah's prior life. Nearly nothing is provided to us in the Bible about what kind of ministry Jonah had prior to being called to go to Nineveh. And the book of Jonah itself tells us nothing about Jonah's life, background, qualifications, or even his lineage except to say that he was the *son of Amittai.*

Little is actually known about Jonah outside of what we read in his book. But Second Kings 14:23–25 tells us that Jonah, son of Amittai, was a prophet from Gath-hepher, a town in the northern part of ancient Israel. We also read in that passage that Jonah spoke for the Lord when foretelling an event that later was fulfilled by the king of Israel, Jeroboam II, son of Jehoash.

That's all the background information we're provided about the prophet in the biblical record outside of the book of Jonah.

But as the story in the book of Jonah unfolds, we eventually gain significant insight into the man, the prophet, the preacher named Jonah. And that will be seen as we progress through the pages of this book.

As we begin, I affirm to you my belief that the words of Scripture themselves are our most sure guide in correctly dividing the words of truth, and I'll do my very best to stay within the bounds of what the Bible tells us and not allow my interests in particular topics to draw me away from what can be supported by what the Bible reveals. If I speculate on something, I'll let you know I'm doing it; and you can be the judge of how you feel about my thoughts.

So what can we glean from the story of Jonah? We begin our harvest in the very first sentence in the book. Here is where we start our search for answers about how much God cares. But let's prepare ourselves for that by first looking much farther back in history.

People who are known as *Deists* promote a view that God is our creator, and He should be respected as such. However, they also promote a belief (Deism) that once our world was put in motion, God went away to basically allow us to fend for ourselves among the forces of nature that He established.

Deists believe God is not interested in being involved in any ongoing fashion in the affairs of His creation on earth. But according to what we read in the Bible, our creator is most assuredly engaged in our world. And He always has been.

The Bible infers that at one time God actually, commonly, walked with Adam and Eve in the garden that He made for them to inhabit and care for.

> *When the cool evening breezes were blowing, the man and his wife heard the* LORD *God walking about in the garden. So they hid from the* LORD *God among the trees. Then the* LORD *God called to the man, "Where are you?"*
>
> *He replied, "I heard you walking in the garden, so I hid. I was afraid because I was naked."* (Genesis 3:8–10)

From even the story of Creation, we see God both caring about people and calling out to them—even after they entered a sinful state of being.

We were made by God. Knowing and accepting that will affect everything about our existence if we'll just internalize it and not let the teachings of godless evolutionists persuade us to think otherwise. And what we read in the Bible systematically demonstrates that the very fact we are God's creation motivates Him to be involved in our lives.

The Lord wants fellowship with us, and He wants to speak to us. He calls out to us. But from what we see in only this one quoted passage taken from early in Genesis, the response of people to God's call is not always what He wants to hear.

We see communication problems arising between the Lord and mankind even in this first written account of Him calling and people answering. And in the case of this first-recorded response of humans to God's first-recorded call to sinners, we understand the decisions made by Adam and Eve caused them to feel shame. And that shame caused them—as sinners—to want to avoid contact with their creator.

Because of their own decisions, their thought patterns had quickly begun to differ from those instilled in them by the Creator. Their eyes suddenly saw things differently, and they understood things in a way God had not intended.

Before Adam and Eve became ashamed to present themselves before the Lord, they first allowed their thoughts to become self-centered. They put their own desires and their own reasoning above God's instructions, and that led them to disobey Him by eating the fruit of the one tree withheld from them by their all-knowing creator—withheld from them for their own good.

Adam and Eve allowed their minds to become swayed into thinking that God was treating them unfairly by keeping from them something that to them seemed good. They convinced themselves that eating the forbidden fruit of the tree was the right thing to do.

They believed they were justified to think the way they did. But through their act of disobedience, they proved themselves wrong, and they inherited a life of hardship and suffering never intended for them to know.

Others may explain this another way, but basically, Adam's and Eve's disobedience grew out of them allowing their thinking to disagree with God's.

So thus it began; that is, so began our historical struggle with human inabilities to consistently and willingly answer God's calls in positive and healthy ways. And so also began mankind's struggle to agree with the Lord and understand the truth of things as *He* sees it.

Moving on from there as we continue to prepare ourselves for handling all we find in the book of Jonah, consider this: Before the call that God made to Adam and Eve on such a sad day in the garden, the Creator already knew they had a problem. He knew what they did. It wasn't hidden from Him. And note that even though they disobeyed God, He was not motivated toward destroying them.

God still wanted to walk with them. He still wanted a close relationship with them. He still wanted to talk with them. And from that time in human history, the Lord began illustrating that even though there is a price to pay for disobeying Him, He is interested in finding solutions for the disobedient.

God wants to restore broken fellowship.

But even more, for some reason that no one can adequately explain, God desires to be with and commune with His creation even when a part of that creation becomes His enemy. And we'll consider that in some detail later in our study of Jonah.

It's no secret that the Lord found joy and fulfillment through His involvement with all of His creation; for in the story of Creation we read again and again that God looked upon what He made and saw *it was good.*[1] That means God was pleased with every part of it, and seeing what He created brought Him a sense of satisfaction.

---

1 Genesis chapter one.

But the Lord was concerned more about Adam and Eve than all the rest of what He made. Adam and Eve were the ones made in His image. They were the ones made to have a unique relationship with Him not enjoyed by any other part of Creation. So perhaps we can try to imagine the concern and heartbreak God felt when they didn't show up for their walk with Him.

One can imagine that before sin entered into their lives, Adam and Eve normally went to meet God, their friend and creator, whenever they "*heard the Lord God walking about in the garden.*" But they didn't show up that time. Adam and Eve had both sinned, and that caused them to act out mankind's first instance of avoidance.

Perhaps we should pause to realize the Creator could have just wrapped things up right then and there. He could have just eliminated His first attempt to make an earthly family and started over afresh. It would have been easy for Him to do. But He didn't. Instead, He began demonstrating His love for Creation by going to the trouble of addressing Adam's and Eve's issue.

And following that, God began to reveal to us in Scripture a very long and patient plan to redeem Creation. And His plan was one that would personally cost Him dearly.

God's first call, and how He dealt with the first people to disobey and disappoint Him, begin to reveal to us how much God cares, but that indeed merely introduces us to the extent of God's care and concern for His creation. We'll learn much more about that from the book of Jonah.

God's call to Adam and Eve was His first call to anyone recorded in the Bible, but it was just the beginning. And in every instance when a call from God was recorded in Scripture, God had a good reason to call. Each and every one of His calls was purposeful, planned in advance, and important to Him; so it's not surprising that He always expected people to answer Him when they heard His voice.

We read in the Bible that many of the people the Lord called agreed with His intentions and responded to His voice with positive replies. But most definitely, some did not.

And such was the response Jonah gave to God.

Much more about that is coming up. For now, though, we'll start our study with God looking down from heaven in the days of Jonah to observe what was going on in the Middle East. When He did, He saw many problems that needed to be addressed. And among them was the great city of Nineveh, the largest city in the Assyrian empire.

Nineveh had become a vile, wicked place, and it came to the point that God decided to do something about it. He decided that He'd had enough of the evil He observed among the Assyrians, and He was going to act against them. He determined to bring judgment their way.

As most people experience problems caused by those who oppose them and their plans, it's natural—the way of the world—for them to want to strike out and deal with those problems quickly if they have the power to do so. And if we who live in the flesh were to have the same unlimited power that God possesses, it's highly likely that many of us, if not most of us, would take swift action to do away with the problems our enemies cause us by doing away with the source of the problems.

I'm speaking of the tendencies of the flesh here, which we should all comprehend. Drive a stake down by this thought as we move toward a better understanding of what is revealed in the book of Jonah.

So truthfully, if we had been in God's position of dealing with Nineveh—but were still bound to fleshly attitudes and passions—it's highly likely that we would have made short work of the Ninevites and not looked back. But we find in our reading of Jonah's story that God ended up being both patient and forgiving when it came to His dealings with them.

When I consider that, I can't help but be impressed by God—knowing that He, who has all power to do anything He wants, could be so patient and tolerant (as we know He is) toward people who oppose Him and live wicked lives.

God could have expressed His displeasure with the people of Nineveh by destroying them as He did with Sodom, Gomorrah, and the cities of the plains in the days of Abraham.[2] Things can get to the place where the Lord's sense of justice moves Him to take that kind of action. But the Bible shows us the Creator's grace and love for His creation far outpace His desire for retribution and justice.

While we may be more interested in *getting rid* of problems, God is more interested in *fixing* them.

The Lord is more interested in healing than killing. He would rather forgive people by bringing them to repentance

---

2 Genesis chapters 18 and 19.

than cast them away from Him. God is more motivated toward saving people from destruction than destroying them—even if the process of saving them causes both Him and His own followers a great deal of trouble.

So when the wickedness of Nineveh came up before Him (moved Him to action), what did God do? Did he organize an army of His people to deal with them or bring against them a military force from some other nation to punish them? Did He send fire down from heaven upon them?

Did God cause the earth to shake violently, open up, and swallow them? Did He drown them in a flood? Or did He himself lead an army of angels to defeat them and bring them to their knees (which He certainly could have done)?

No!

What did He do then? What did God in His wisdom decide to do? What became His plan to deal with Nineveh? Surely the Lord cared enough about what was going on there to take action. The Assyrians were terribly violent and wicked, and history reveals they deserved God's retribution. Surely He would do something to show He cared about that!

What did the Creator do to prove He cared enough to deal with the Ninevites? The book of Jonah shows us that God cared enough about what was going on in Nineveh—He cared enough about how the wickedness of the Ninevites was affecting the world—to call one person to help Him bring about the solution He devised for dealing with them.

It's not my purpose to explain why God chooses to do everything He does. And I don't intend to spend time apologizing for His decisions to often deal through others instead of taking care of things himself, directly—without a man's or a woman's assistance. I simply acknowledge and accept His choice.

Truly, the Creator of the Universe, who merely speaks things into existence, doesn't actually need our meager efforts and abilities to accomplish anything. Nothing forces Him to depend on our assistance in carrying out His business, but He chooses to involve us in what He's doing. And that is all the explanation of His reasoning for choosing to call men and women to action on His behalf that we need to go into.

When it comes to calling people to perform a task in His name, He has both the right to do it and the right to determine *when* to do it. But in addition to that, God also has the right to demand the obedience of those whom He calls. The Lord calls people and expects them to follow His instructions.

When God calls, sometimes people immediately launch out in faith to do the Lord's bidding. Other people, though, answer His call but obey Him grudgingly and drag their feet. And still others entirely and knowingly refuse to do what God calls them to do and pay a price for their disobedience.

Jonah, unfortunately, fell into the last category.

Many people discount the importance of the callings that God places upon His followers, but they should never underestimate the significance of what the Lord is doing when He appoints people to work or speak for Him. Jonah, like others before him, was being called to an important work. God in His wisdom determined that he was the right person to go to Nineveh and deliver to its citizens His pronouncement of judgment.

We can imagine Jonah was simply going about his normal business the day the Lord called—whatever business that was. But that day proved to be unlike any others for him. What happened on that day affected his life in ways he could never have fathomed. That day, he received a particularly important call from God.

The Lord spoke to Jonah and told him He had a job for him to do. And it was time for him to do it—right away!

"Jonah," God said, *"Get up and go to the great city of Nineveh. Announce my judgment against it."*

God cares enough to call a preacher.

CHAPTER 2

GOD CARES ENOUGH TO BE LONGSUFFERING

But Jonah got up and went in the opposite direction to get away from the L*ORD.* (Jonah 1:3a)

GOD SPOKE TO Jonah and told him to go to Nineveh and preach. Jonah was then faced with a decision. He needed to decide what to do about it. God's call required a response from Jonah, and we'll examine his response in a moment. Before we do, though, we'll attempt to better position our hearts for dealing with it.

In order for us to learn the right lessons from the book of Jonah, we need to deliberately handle Jonah's response with a sense of humility. We'll overlook the full message of the book if we become overly judgmental.

As we deal with Jonah's answer to God's call, we'll start by giving some thought to how we handle our own decisions to do the Lord's bidding. That will help us bring things into proper perspective when examining Jonah's response.

There are people who with confidence believe if they were to hear God speak to them in a dramatic way, and if He were to give them personal instructions to do this or that, they would of course do the Lord's bidding. In other words, they assume they definitely would never be like Jonah. But could they be overconfident?

Before we get too wrapped up in criticizing Jonah's response to God, we'll conduct a short self-examination to help us relate at least in some way to his thoughts and actions.

Ask yourself, "Have I always followed God's instructions?"

"Have I always responded with a ready willingness to work for Him and let Him direct me?"

"In doing what the Lord requires of me, have I always done things with a proper attitude?"

"Is there any chance that I, like others, could allow myself to form some kind of excuse for not doing the Lord's will because His request sounds unreasonable? Can I really be so bold as to say I would never move contrary to God's will like Jonah?"

If we're honest, many if not most of us (all of us?) have had God speak to us in one way or another and failed to give Him a positive response and do what He asked us to do. But of course we could have couched our failure in a feeling that we couldn't discern if it was God who was actually speaking to us at the time.

God has heard that before.

Surely if God would speak to us in an audible voice, we wouldn't refuse His call. Right?

If He chooses to, the Lord can certainly reveal himself to us in an authoritative, verbal manner that is unambiguous even to the flesh. But most often He tends to lead and direct His people through the whispers of the Holy Spirit.

Hearing the soft-spoken instructions of the Holy Spirit is usually enough for those who are in tune with God's spirit and listening for Him to speak. Frankly, if we don't respond to such instructions and believe we can wait for God to reveal himself to us audibly or in a more demonstrable way before accepting and following His directions, we have little to no excuse for that kind of thinking.

There are of course times when it's perfectly fine to ask God to do something to give us confidence that He's calling us to a task. For example, in chapter six of the book of Judges, Gideon asked the Lord for signs to confirm His will when the Lord called him to rescue the Israelites from the Midianites. But as we read that account in Scripture, we find no indication that Gideon harbored an attitude that inclined him toward refusing to do God's will.

Gideon had reservations about his own abilities, and He asked God for assurances that he was walking in His will. He asked for signs to confirm what the Lord was telling him, but he didn't attempt to avoid his calling by coming up with some kind of excuse to evade the responsibilities placed upon him by God.

The task given to Gideon was what I refer to as a *special calling*. That is, it was similar to the task God gave to Jonah. God was calling one person to perform a special task. We're about to dig further into Jonah's response to his special calling, but first, let's continue to prepare ourselves by going beyond reflecting on that to consider the willingness—or perhaps I should say, unwillingness—of people to respond even to our *common callings.*

Our Lord has already spoken to vast numbers of people—actually to all of us—in various ways, and most people are ignoring Him every day. He has already called out to everyone through the words of Scripture and His actions throughout history. God has already revealed himself and His general call and will for all of mankind.

Without doubt, we all have a common calling to come to Christ for our salvation. And we all have a common calling to follow Him in Christian service.

The Creator has revealed himself, His will, His overarching desires, and His common demands to both believer *and* nonbeliever.[3] And especially when it comes to the Lord's followers, the call in the Bible for all Christians to participate in the Great Commission is clear. But is every Christian doing what God has called us to do by participating in that work?

Hardly!

We all have an obligation to respond to what God has spoken and already revealed in Scripture. His will revealed to us in Scripture applies to us even if we feel we have never had the Lord speak to us personally or give us more specific directions. And speaking for the Church in general, we certainly have *not* always responded to God's will in a positive way.

---

3 "But God shows his anger from heaven against all sinful, wicked people who suppress the truth by their wickedness. They know the truth about God because he has made it obvious to them. For ever since the world was created, people have seen the earth and sky. Through everything God made, they can clearly see his invisible qualities—his eternal power and divine nature. So they have no excuse for not knowing God" (Romans 1:18–20).

When the Word of God—the ultimate *Truth*[4]—is preached, taught, or promoted to people in any manner, those who hear or read that truth are responsible for reacting to it. And for sure, people don't always react properly.

People often dismiss the ministry of truth, and they're responsible for that dismissal. Truth may be denied, but it cannot be avoided forever. It will outlast all unbelief and all the attempts to evade it. Truth will one day sit in judgment over the past responses of all people. It will last forever. And like truth, God's calls—regardless of being either special or common—are also lasting and beyond our ability to alter.

Considering the population of our planet and spiritual conditions worldwide, the majority of people who live on the face of the earth today are living in disobedience to God's call in one way or another. Most are living lives of avoidance when it comes to His plans for them.

Undeniably, most of the world's populace—who actually make no attempt to follow Jesus at all—have failed to accept the Creator's claims on their lives. But we must never allow ourselves to get the idea that acts of avoidance or disobedience can be committed only by non-Christians.

Sadly, people in the Church—believers, followers of Christ, those who know God—are also found to sidestep the will of God and disobey Him. Even believers all too often fall into living lives of avoidance and make excuses for not following God's directions.

---

4 John 1:1–14

Christians can, without doubt, indeed find themselves attempting to shift the blame onto God for their lack of involvement in the work and mission of the Church by convincing themselves they are simply waiting for the Lord to personally speak to them and give them directions.

How foolish!

The Bible already reveals God's general marching orders to all Christians. We have already been commissioned to carry His Word to the world and make disciples.[5] His revealed will is for all believers to be faithful servants who are inviting people to the banquet the Lord has prepared for them to enjoy.[6]

People who are *waiting to hear from God* before they actively involve themselves in the missional or evangelistic work of the Church are fooling themselves. They're mistaken to think they can escape the Great Commission by ignoring it or pretending it doesn't apply to them.

By discounting the responsibilities already placed upon the Church (capitalized Church, all believers), those who ignore our common callings are failing to respond obediently to the Creator's will for them. And by doing that—similar to unbelievers who fail to accept God's claim on their lives—they are

---

5 "Therefore, go and make disciples of all the nations, baptizing them in the name of the Father and the Son and the Holy Spirit. Teach these new disciples to obey all the commands I have given you" (Matthew 28:19–20a).

6 "And he said to his servants, 'The wedding feast is ready, and the guests I invited aren't worthy of the honor. Now go out to the street corners and invite everyone you see.' So the servants brought in everyone they could find, good and bad alike, and the banquet hall was filled with guests" (Matthew 22:8–10).

in all reality attempting to hide or run away from God and His call to them.

And while hiding is forever linked to Adam, running away from God leads us directly to Jonah.

Be honest as we approach learning about Jonah's attitudes and experiences. Admit it; we are flesh just as Jonah was flesh. And as flesh, we can falsely claim that God has not spoken to us and made His will clear to us—when He has. But beyond that, like Jonah, *we* can even know beyond a shadow of doubt what God wants us to do and still refuse to do it.

Scripture tells us that Jonah *got up* after hearing God's call and *went in the opposite direction* from where the Lord wanted him to go—in the opposite direction of the way to Nineveh. The New King James Version says Jonah fled to Tarshish *"from the presence of the Lord."* And in doing so, he was running away from his responsibility to do what God called him to do.

But the truth is, Jonah couldn't really run away from God; He is omnipresent. That means the Creator has the ability to be (possesses the actual attribute of being) everywhere. In simple terms, if we're running away from God, when we get to where we're going, regardless of where we go, we will find that He is already there waiting for us to arrive.

We will never be successful in any attempt to avoid responsibility by running from God.

It matters not where we go; we can run anywhere, and the result will be the same. Attempting to run away from God is an act of futility. And Jonah was soon going to find that out.

This early in the narrative, we have not yet been told what actually motivated Jonah to attempt to run away from the Lord—or away from the responsibility placed upon him. We'll learn that later. All we know at this point in the book of Jonah is that his actions revealed he decided *not* to do what God asked him to do.

Deciding not to do what God wants is a terrible thing, of course. But as mentioned before, make the conscious decision to treat Jonah's action with humility. For just as I already inferred, both unbelievers and believers alike are tempted to disobey God and often do. And both are prone to react in similar ways even if not in the same way or to the same degree as Jonah.

"But Jonah was a man of God, a prophet!" some will exclaim. "That makes it different."

Does it really?

Admittedly, even though Jonah doesn't have a high profile in the Bible compared to some other preachers and prophets—those like Elijah, Jeremiah, and Isaiah—it's still significant to realize that Jonah was, indeed, a man of God who had been appointed to represent the Lord before the people. And his work was no less important than that of any other prophet in God's view.

Jonah is among those in the Bible known as *minor prophets.* That actually only means the books written by or about those so classified are short in their content compared to the larger books by other prophets. So yes, he was indeed a prophet.

"But this is terrible!" they will say. "Surely a prophet, a preacher, a man of God, should never fail to follow God's call!"

Yes, but . . .

"Why, if a preacher can fail to heed and obey God, what chance do I have of not failing God?"

Such sentiment is common, but Christians who are mature and thoroughly equipped for every good work[7] will understand that all men are, well, men. And by the way, all women are, well, women.

We're all flesh and subject to temptations and frailties. We all need both God's grace and the power inherent in the blood of Christ to live faithful and obedient lives. And we all—preacher and lay person alike—must repent and return to faithfully following Christ if and when we fail at any time to live up to God's expectations.

Thank God for His matchless grace and favor! We're going to learn a lot more about grace and favor as we go through this study.

So try to be understanding with Jonah. He was a man with a problem. And in fact, God *knew* Jonah had a problem when He called him to travel and preach to Nineveh. Pay close attention to this if you are someone who thinks a person must be perfect and entirely pleasing to God before the Lord can call and use that person to do His will.

Before we finish studying the book of Jonah, it will become evident—as clear as crystal in fact—that God was willing to go the extra mile when dealing with Nineveh. We'll come face to face with the magnitude of the Lord's desire to save the lost.

7 2 Timothy 3:16–17.

But while God's patience with the lost will be something most Christians should be able to wrap their minds around, perhaps it won't be so easy for some to even want to think about, much less talk about, God's intent and fortitude to address and heal a bad relationship that can develop between the Lord and a preacher—or between the Lord and any other Christian who is running from Him.

As we continue our study of the book of Jonah, we'll come to understand that our Creator is revealed to be patient and determined when dealing with *all* of us—with anyone who practices disobedience or walks contrary to His will.

Place that firmly in your mind.

Even as Jonah was running away from the Lord, even as he was rejecting his personal calling, God was not ready to give up on him, cast him aside, and move on.

Yes, God cares enough to be longsuffering.

CHAPTER 3

GOD CARES ENOUGH TO SEND A STORM

He went down to the port of Joppa, where he found a ship leaving for Tarshish. He bought a ticket and went on board, hoping to escape from the Lord *by sailing to Tarshish. But the* Lord *hurled a powerful wind over the sea, causing a violent storm that threatened to break the ship apart.* (Jonah 1:3b–4)

TO PUT IT MILDLY, Jonah didn't like God's call. There was no question in his mind what God was calling him to do. He simply did NOT want to do it. Jonah didn't just fail in some way as he went about trying to fulfill the Lord's will; he didn't just drag his feet; he purposely decided to disobey God by running away from responsibility.

Instead of at least reluctantly moving toward doing the Lord's will, Jonah decided to go to the port city of Joppa (now part of Tel Aviv) and pay for passage on a ship that was bound for Tarshish. And take note of this: According to multiple authorities, Tarshish was a city in southwestern Spain! That means Jonah indeed made a conscious decision to go as far as he possibly could *in the opposite direction* from the way to Nineveh, a city located in what is now northern Iraq.

But as it's said, the best laid plans of mice and men often go awry,[8] and Jonah's trip didn't go as he wanted.

Jonah had to have known that he could not actually be successful in running from God and his responsibility—his calling. But he also had to have been absolutely intent on disobeying the Lord, and we'll understand the reason for that as we continue our study.

He didn't want to do what God called him to do, and it seems that, like a child throwing a temper tantrum, he was intent on getting his way no matter the cost.

All seemed to be going well at first. Jonah boarded the ship, and he and the ship's crew cast off from the shore in comfortable waters. But such conditions were not to last. We have no way of knowing how long the ship was at sea, but they were likely far from shore and perhaps long into their voyage when the storm developed.

The clouds gathered, and the wind started blowing. A violent storm developed, and the ship's crew fought to keep the ship and its cargo secure. But the storm grew so severe that it looked like the ship could break up and sink.

According to the book of Jonah, all the sailors were in a panic. They all started praying to whatever gods they trusted, and as conditions worsened, they began lightening the load on the ship by tossing cargo overboard (v. 5). Of course without delivering their precious cargo in Spain, they would earn no livelihood; but they likely knew that losing the cargo was the only chance they had of saving their own lives.

---

8 Original: "The best laid schemes o' mice an' men gang aft a-gley"—from the poem *To a Mouse* by Robert Burns, 1786.

As the crew fought to keep the ship afloat, the captain of the ship eventually went below deck, where he found Jonah fast asleep.

> *"How can you sleep at a time like this?" he shouted. "Get up and pray to your god! Maybe he will pay attention to us and spare our lives."* (Jonah 1:6b)

In the captain's opinion, there was no need at that time to argue about whose god was the true God. In fact, to him, I'm sure any god would do if that god could stop the storm and save them. *More people, praying to more gods, the better* was probably his opinion.

Isn't it amazing that Jonah could be sleeping at a time like that? Maybe he felt comfortable and perhaps even justified with his decision to run from God. It seems that not even a storm that threatened his life and all the others onboard concerned him enough to keep him awake.

Or perhaps he felt like whatever happened during his voyage away from responsibility would just happen, and he was simply resigned to receiving whatever misery that came his way. In other words, maybe his attitude was fatalistic since he knew he was disobeying God in a blatant manner. Perhaps he had simply come to be both consumed by and satisfied with a pessimistic view of his future.

Maybe Jonah was prepared to accept and live a cynical life without hope. It's possible he had come to believe that whatever came his way in the future would merely become his justly-earned reward for disobeying God.

Perhaps he was willing to accept any fate—even his own destruction—rather than preach to the people of Nineveh.

> *Then the crew cast lots to see which of them had offended the gods and caused the terrible storm. When they did this, the lots identified Jonah as the culprit.* (Jonah 1:7)

Casting lots—that sounds like a strange way to find an answer from God. To us today, it sounds awfully superstitious, doesn't it? We clearly wouldn't want to decide all of life's issues based on casting lots, but there does seem to be a time and place for it.

There are actually many instances recorded in the Bible when lots were cast to determine between certain choices. Even the disciples of Christ cast lots to determine God's will in an issue. They felt the need to find a replacement for the disciple Judas, who had committed suicide after betraying Jesus to His enemies.

After choosing two men who were good candidates for the position, it seems the disciples couldn't decide between the two, so they prayed and cast lots to finally settle the question.

> *Then they all prayed, "O Lord, you know every heart. Show us which of these men you have chosen as an apostle to replace Judas in this ministry, for he has deserted us and gone where he belongs."* (Acts 1:24–25)

The lot fell to one named Matthias, and he became one of the twelve initial leaders in the Church. They trusted God to make the decision. They trusted Him to control how the lots fell, and He didn't disappoint them. The disciples were not leaving the choice up to chance; they left it up to God.

Again, we certainly wouldn't want to depend on casting lots when making all important decisions, but we should always believe in the ability of God to reveal His will one way or another.

When necessary, then, there is a precedent for trusting God to reveal the truth through casting lots; and revealing truth is exactly what the Lord did when the sailors cast lots on that ship as it was violently tossing to and fro in the midst of an angry Mediterranean Sea.

They cast lots, and the lot fell to reveal Jonah as the one who caused God to bring the storm upon them.

> *"Why has this awful storm come down on us?" they demanded. "Who are you? What is your line of work? What country are you from? What is your nationality?"*
>
> *Jonah answered, "I am a Hebrew, and I worship the LORD, the God of heaven, who made the sea and the land."*
>
> *The sailors were terrified when they heard this, for he had already told them he was running away from the LORD. "Oh, why did you do it?" they groaned.* (Jonah 1:8–10)

The ship's crew and captain then knew the source of their calamity, but that didn't solve their problem. The ship continued to pitch from side to side and rise and fall with the violent waves. The wind continued to howl and rip the sails. The masts were likely breaking by that time, and they were left with rowing as their only hope of moving the ship.

Clearly the sailors came to respect the God from whom Jonah was running, and they respected Jonah for knowing God's will; for they then asked Jonah what they should do to make the sea calm down. They were ready to do whatever Jonah told them the Lord required (v. 11).

Jonah knew what to do.

"Throw me into the sea," Jonah said, "and it will become calm again. I know that this terrible storm is all my fault."

(Jonah 1:12)

The ship's crew had their answer, but they seem to have been honorable men who valued not only their own lives but also the lives of others in their care. So instead of obeying the Lord's advice just given through Jonah (imagine God still speaking through that man), they attempted to continue to row even harder toward land.

But then the storm got even worse. "*The sea continued to grow more tempestuous against them*" (Jonah 1:13b NKJV). And through that, it seems God was sending the sailors a strong message.

Then they cried out to the LORD, Jonah's God. "O LORD," they pleaded, "don't make us die for this man's sin. And don't hold us responsible for his death. O LORD, you have sent this storm upon him for your own good reasons." (Jonah 1:14)

No longer were the sailors praying randomly to this or that god, they were praying to Jonah's God, the one true God, Creator of the Universe. The men began believing in the authority of God because of the words of a disobedient preacher. Then because of Jonah's words and what the Lord had revealed to them through the storm, they finally responded by doing what God wanted them to do.

When they finished praying, they threw Jonah into the violent waves. And once Jonah was off the ship, the winds laid, and according to Scripture, the "*storm stopped at once*" (v. 15).

As far as what happened to the ship's captain and crew after that, I assume they were able to finally row the ship to the nearest shore, and perhaps it was there where they offered a sacrifice to Jonah's very active, powerful, and merciful God.

> *The sailors were awestruck by the LORD's great power, and they offered him a sacrifice and vowed to serve him.* (Jonah 1:16)

In times of trouble, pain, or sorrow, people sometimes wonder where God is. They wonder if God cares. Throughout the book of Jonah we find out how much He really does.

The Lord wanted Jonah to warn the Ninevites about what was going to happen to them. He cared greatly about the appointed task Jonah refused to perform. And God cared enough about it to deal directly and powerfully with the preacher who was running from his calling.

But beyond that, in dealing with Jonah, God used His actions to do even more. The Lord knows how to get more value out of any one deed performed by either Him or His followers than we can ever anticipate. The storm God sent was His first major action in dealing with Jonah. But He also used that same storm to bring to Him a whole ship-load of sailors (and notably—hold this thought—likely all gentiles).

Because the Lord is indeed always good, some people portray Him as doing only "good things" as judged in the eyes of men. They can never allow themselves to see God as responsible for anything we are prone to interpret as "bad." And because of their views, instead of at least questioning if God could be causing or allowing something bad, troubling, or challenging to come along in their lives for His purpose—they will automatically blame the devil or some other opposing or evil force for it.

Many people look immediately to the devil's actions or anyone else's activities but their own as the cause of their discomfort, pain, or trouble. They don't even pause to consider whether or not their own thoughts, actions, or responses to the Lord could have had something to do with either causing their problem or requiring God to bring trouble or challenging experiences into their lives to correct and teach them.

People's beliefs or theology can cause them to overlook reality. They can become entirely blind to the type or extent of God's involvement in times of trouble and what He is trying to do in their lives. Such people need to seriously study and accept what God teaches us through the book of Jonah.

I'm clearly not encouraging people to accuse God of causing every "bad" thing that comes their way. That's certainly not true. After all, we are indeed involved in a spiritual battle against Satan and the forces of evil. But we have a need to exercise discernment and wisdom in the midst of our battles with either outside forces or those within. And wisdom is not found in avoiding reality and truth.

Just as God brought trouble upon Jonah to speak to his heart and minister truth to him, He is still absolutely able and willing to do that today for our benefit when necessary. We must be careful not to allow ourselves to form views that darken our understanding of the Creator's dealings with us and the world around us.

Sometimes people fail to realize that God knows about and gets involved in calamities and trouble that arise in the world

He created. He is not simply watching what is happening on earth from afar and refusing to inject himself into our affairs.

People need to understand that regardless of the source of our troubles, God is always active in our lives and uses things as He sees fit to speak to us for our ultimate good.[9] And sadly, sometimes things can get so serious that God himself must purposely and personally take action to cause what we view as "*bad things*" in order for Him to get His point across.

We find in our reading of the book of Jonah that it was God—no one else—who was bringing trouble upon Jonah for his disobedience. We also find that Jonah knew exactly the source of his trouble. And as we continue reading, we'll see that all of the things Jonah experienced from the hand of God were leading him to acknowledge truth and encouraging him to change some of his deeply-seated views.

Finally, when we consider the prayer of the ship's crew recorded for us—a prayer by those who before that day did not know the Lord—it's clear that even those sailors realized the Creator had a good reason to do what He did.

So yes, if it becomes necessary, God cares enough to send a storm.

---

9 "And we know that God causes everything to work together for the good of those who love God and are called according to his purpose for them" (Romans 8:28).

CHAPTER 4

GOD CARES ENOUGH TO PROVIDE A FISH

Now the LORD had arranged for a great fish to swallow Jonah.
(Jonah 1:17a)

THERE HAS LONG been plenty of speculation about this part of the story. Many people have questioned the ability of Jonah, or anyone else for that matter, to not simply be swallowed by a big fish but also stay in what is commonly referred to as the *belly of the whale* for days and live to tell about it.

But the Bible declares the fish existed and retrieved the fleeing preacher from beneath the waves of the sea by swimming up to Jonah and swallowing him.

The New King James Version reads, "*the LORD had prepared a great fish.*" The Amplified Bible reads, "*the LORD had prepared (appointed, destined) a great fish.*"

In order to either defend or discount the Bible's narrative about Jonah being swallowed by a great fish, and it spitting him out alive days later, many people have spent considerable energy and time researching and writing about the potential, physical possibilities of the event.

Regardless of whether or not they actually believe the story of Jonah, most people have assumed it had to have been a whale that God provided to swallow him. Of course that's based on the fact that whales are among the largest of sea animals, with the Blue Whale being the largest animal now swimming in any of the world's oceans.

But there are large fish other than whales, and one of them could have been a candidate for being used by God as the great Jonah-swallower. In fact, according to an article by Donald H. Harrison posted on the web site, *JewishSightSeeing.com,* on September 13, 2002, two officials at *Sea World* in San Diego, California, came to the conclusion that a *great white shark* could have been the best suspect.[10]

According to them, a *great white* has both a mouth and esophagus large enough to swallow a man. And great whites routinely dine on large sea animals such as big elephant seals. But that's not all that led the officials to propose Jonah's "fish" could have been a great white shark.

You see, one issue of contention, especially for those who discount Jonah's story, has been the idea that a person could spend days in the belly of a fish without being digested. And a shark could be a better choice for swallowing and not digesting Jonah since warm-blooded mammals, like whales, have faster digestive systems than cold-blooded animals like sharks.

But then there is another issue to deal with—the issue of an individual having enough oxygen to breathe while in the belly of a fish.

---

10 http://www.jewishsightseeing.com/usa/california/san_diego/general_stories/sd9-13-02jonah.html, accessed March 25, 2023.

Fanciful pictures have been drawn of how Jonah can be imagined to have not only been conscious but certainly breathing as he knelt to pray or lounged against the side of a whale's belly. There is, of course, nothing in the story of Jonah to indicate that he had any way to move around or kneel to pray while submerged inside the fish. But if he was able to breathe while there, how?

While ocean mammals like whales are capable of taking in a great deal of air when they occasionally surface to breathe, there is no proven explanation of how that fresh air could make its way to their bellies. No one has been able to come up with a satisfying, biological explanation of how Jonah could have sufficient oxygen to breathe during his days-long imprisonment in the deep.

There are fish large enough to swallow a man. There are fish large enough to pass a bite the size of a man through their esophagus to their stomach in one gulp. There are fish that would be better-suited to holding a man in their stomachs for days without completely digesting him, but how would the man breathe? Is it physically possible for a man to have enough oxygen to live in the belly of a fish for more than a few minutes?

Before we move on to the conclusion I want to leave with you on this topic, I'll mention another item that has been recorded about men's experiences with giant sea life.

In 1931, an account was published in Ripley's publication *Believe It Or Not*,[11] in which was recorded the experience of

11 Ripley Entertainment Inc., 7576 Kingspointe Pkwy–Suite 188, Orlando, FL 32819

James Bartley, a sailor who was said to have been swallowed by a whale and lived to tell his story. The Ripley account contained a translation of an article published in the *Journal des Debats* and written by the journal's scientific editor, M. de Parville, who recorded the account in 1914.

Following is that account, and an internet search on "M. de Parville" or "modern Jonah" will reveal it has been republished in several places.

> In February 1891, the whaling ship "Star of the East" was in the vicinity of the Falkland Islands when the lookout sighted a large sperm whale 3 miles away. Two boats were launched, and in a short time one of the harpooners was enabled to spear the whale.
>
> The second boat attacked the whale but was upset by a lash of its tail, and the men were thrown into the sea, one man being drowned; and another, James Bartley, could not be found.
>
> The whale was killed in a few hours—its great body lying on the ship's side, while the crew busied itself with axes and spades removing the blubber. They worked all day and part of the night.
>
> The next morning they attached some tackle to the stomach of the whale and hoisted it on deck. Suddenly, the sailors were startled by something in it which gave spasmodic signs of life. Inside was found the missing sailor doubled up and unconscious.
>
> He was placed on deck and treated to a bath of sea water, which soon revived him, but his mind was not clear, and

> he was placed in the captain's quarters, where he remained for two weeks a raving lunatic.
>
> He was kindly and carefully treated by the captain and the ship's officers and gradually regained possession of his senses. At the end of the third week he entirely recovered from the shock and resumed his duties.
>
> During the sojourn in the whale's stomach, Bartley's skin, where it was exposed to the action of the gastric juices, underwent a striking change. His face, neck, and hands were bleached to a deadly whiteness, taking on the appearance of parchment.
>
> Bartley remembered the lash of the whale's tail and then was encompassed by great darkness, and he felt that he was slipping along a smooth passage that seemed to move and carry him forward. His hands came in contact with a yielding, slimy substance, which seemed to shrink from his touch.
>
> He could easily breathe, but the heat was terrible. It seemed to open the pores of his skin and draw out his vitality. The next he remembered, he was in the captain's cabin. While he recovered fully from his mental depression, his skin retained its ghastly pallor to the end and never recovered its natural appearance.

After repeating the above account, I'll also say there are those who have found problems with it. For instance, researcher Edward B. Davis, Ph.D., in a paper available online, claims evidence that whaling was not conducted in the vicinity of the Falkland Islands until 1909.[12]

Also in the article written by Dr. Davis, he presents evidence that the crew register for that cruise of the Star of the East did not include a sailor named James Bartley. And of note, Dr. Davis did not present his evidence to try disproving the Bible's record of Jonah's story.

My position is that the story of James Bartley is interesting in context with the biblical narrative, but it is not needed for proving the truth of Jonah's story. I don't feel any pressure to convince anyone about the truth of Jonah's experience based on anybody's research or explanation.

Believe it or not, the Creator of our world doesn't depend on any evidence more currently recorded to prove anything He has done in the past. And His ability to do anything He wants to do even today is not limited by any of the laws of nature.

The Bartley story may be a complete fabrication—and as recorded in a statement Davis found reportedly from the wife of the ship's captain, "a great sea yarn." But that does not detract in any way from the trust I put in the Bible's narrative about Jonah.

Controversy continues today as to the validity of any man being swallowed by a fish and living to relate his story to others. And clearly, what makes the story of Jonah even more unbelievable to many is that he was inside the fish for such an extended time. But in spite of naysayers, and regardless of any arguments or supporting evidence—or lack thereof—I join

---

12 http://www.asa3.org/ASA/PSCF/1991/PSCF12-91Davis.html, accessed March 25, 2023.

others in continuing, adamantly, to believe what the Bible says about Jonah's experiences.

Ultimately, for any Christian who believes in the Holy Spirit's inspiration of Scripture and the authority of the Bible, all it takes to believe the biblical account of Jonah's experience in the deep is for that person to continue trusting the Word of God. It should not be all that difficult for people of faith to believe that God did what the book of Jonah says He did—that what happened to Jonah is absolutely true.

Further, if a person truly believes the biblical account of Creation, it should be easy to believe the biblical account of Jonah's story. It really doesn't matter if the *great fish* the Lord prepared for the task of swallowing Jonah was a great white shark, a whale, or a grouper. God did what the book of Jonah describes.

The Lord prepared a great fish and called upon it to swallow Jonah and carry him along in its stomach as the fish swam through the sea toward its prescribed destination. There really is no reason for a Bible-believing Christian to distrust the Word of God.

Like us, Jonah served the Creator, the great architect, engineer, and builder of the Universe. And if God determined to do so, He could easily have created on that very day a great fish—a one of a kind—created just for the special task of swallowing and keeping Jonah for a time in a watery prison.

Why must the same God who created and instituted the world's natural order of things (through which some people believe everything must be explained and understood) be bound to follow the same rules that He laid down for the procreation of what we know about in nature today?

If God made the world and everything in it, can He not still make anything of His choosing—even one unique, great fish created just for the singular task of scooping up and maintaining the life of a preacher who was running from Him?

God has both the ability and the authority to make anything He wants, even today. He can still make a thousand habitable worlds right now if He chooses. And who are we to say He can't?

Preparing a fish large enough to swallow a *house* would not be a challenge for the Creator if that were to meet His needs. And if He hung our world in space and provided an atmosphere to support all life as we know it, He could just as easily place enough oxygen in the belly of a fish to keep a man breathing for as long as He wants.

The Bible tells us the Lord prepared, or arranged for, a fish to swallow Jonah, and we're called upon to simply believe it. It's not that hard. God isn't limited by either man's lack of understanding or his unwillingness to accept His omnipotence. We must beware of where our pride may take us if we consider ourselves too sophisticated with our own knowledge of things to accept the validity of God's Word.

Jonah ran from God's call. God arranged for a great fish to swallow him. And if we're running from the Lord's wisdom, knowledge, or will for our lives—since He cares about such things—it would be no big thing for the Lord to provide something to swallow us too. This is one of the lessons learned from Jonah's experience.

God cares enough to provide a fish.

CHAPTER 5

GOD CARES ENOUGH TO LISTEN AND SAVE

And Jonah was inside the fish for three days and three nights.

Then Jonah prayed to the LORD his God from inside the fish. He said,

"I cried out to the LORD in my great trouble,
and he answered me.
I called to you from the land of the dead,
and LORD, you heard me!
You threw me into the ocean depths,
and I sank down to the heart of the sea.
The mighty waters engulfed me;
I was buried beneath your wild and stormy waves.
Then I said, 'O LORD, you have driven me from your presence.
Yet I will look once more toward your holy Temple.'

"I sank beneath the waves,
and the waters closed over me.
Seaweed wrapped itself around my head.
I sank down to the very roots of the mountains.

I was imprisoned in the earth,
whose gates lock shut forever.
But you, O Lord my God,
snatched me from the jaws of death!
As my life was slipping away,
I remembered the Lord.
And my earnest prayer went out to you
in your holy Temple.
Those who worship false gods
turn their backs on all God's mercies.
But I will offer sacrifices to you with songs of praise,
and I will fulfill all my vows.
For my salvation comes from the Lord alone."
(Jonah 1:17b–2:9)

AFTER THE SAILORS responded to the Lord's will and threw Jonah into the sea, the great fish prepared by God swallowed him. Nothing is said about what the fish did immediately after that, or where the fish went, but we can surmise it started a three-day journey to take Jonah back to the eastern shores of the Mediterranean.

We've already gathered a lot of information from the book of Jonah, and there have been several actors in this striking but short narrative. There was the man called by God, who acted in disobedience to the Lord's will for him. There was a ship scheduled to depart from Joppa for its voyage to the far-off city of Tarshish. There was a storm. And there were sailors who fought to save the ship as the storm threatened to sink it.

There was the captain who confronted Jonah and along with his crew received and obeyed directions from God —directions clearly given to them through Jonah. Then of course, there was the fish, which has always been the focus of great attention for obvious reasons. Throughout the entire story up to this point, we see that a lot of significant things transpired in a relatively short amount of time.

It should be clear to anyone who receives this story in faith that God was actively orchestrating the events as He responded to Jonah's decisions and those of the ship's crew. It also should not be lost on any of us that the Lord always knows the end from the beginning of all things. And it's evident from the beginning to the end of the story of Jonah that God was firmly in control of the events in every act and scene in the narrative as they unfolded.[13]

But while the Creator always has the ability to control the narrative of any story, we must remember that He chooses to leave many decisions that affect the future up to us (even though He knows the results of our decisions ahead of time). While God always reserves the right to have the final say in history, it is often His choice to merely respond to the choices and decisions He allows us to make. And the decisions made by one man, Jonah, clearly affected the directions this story took.

Think of this: Just as God left it up to Jonah to either obey or disobey His call, He didn't force Jonah to repent from the belly of the fish. Certainly, the Holy Spirit was actively at work in Jonah's heart as God took extraordinary steps to encourage

---

13 "Do not forget this! Keep it in mind! Remember this, you guilty ones. Remember the things I have done in the past. For I alone am God! I am God, and there is none like me. Only I can tell you the future before it even happens. Everything I plan will come to pass, for I do whatever I wish" (Isaiah 46:8–10).

Jonah to see things His way, but it was still up to Jonah to choose his own response to the Holy Spirit's prompting.

Like Pharaoh, who stubbornly refused to let the people leave Egypt,[14] Jonah could have hardened his heart to the Lord's attempts to change his mind. He could have refused to yield to God's will and remained unchanged. It was Jonah's choice.

Even after being tossed into the ocean, Jonah could have maintained a stubborn attitude and clung to a hateful and fatalistic mindset (like I believe he had while still on the ship). And after being swallowed by the fish, he could have succumbed to a final temptation to curse his own life, the world, and God who made it.

But I'm moved to speculate that if God had known Jonah wouldn't repent during his experience, He might not have even prepared a fish for Jonah at all. If the Lord knew that Jonah would not respond to what was coming next—that he would not repent and call out to Him after being swallowed by the fish—perhaps He could have just allowed Jonah to sink to the bottom of the sea, and that would have been the end of it.

After all, while it's clear the Lord was determined for the Ninevites to receive the warning of their impending judgment, if Jonah wouldn't fulfill his calling, God could have turned to someone else to do it. That was certainly His prerogative.

Looking into what developed then from only my vantage point today, I have to assume God knew exactly what it would take to bring Jonah to the only decision that would save his life. The Lord knew it would take Jonah's experience of sliding down into the belly of the fish to soften his heart enough to

14 Exodus 8:32.

cause him to call out to Him. But even with that knowledge, we need to realize the decision was still up to Jonah.

We need to acknowledge that if the experience God arranged had not been enough to move him to repentance, Jonah would have no doubt failed to end up being the preacher God used to carry the Lord's word to Nineveh. He could have just been one fine meal for a hungry fish—a seemingly just end for a rebellious preacher.

But God indeed knew what Jonah's response was going to be even before He called him to go to Nineveh. He knew Jonah would be moved to call out to Him. In God's foreknowledge, He not only knew what steps Jonah would take to refuse his appointment, He knew what kind of fish was required to retrieve him from the deep and take him back in an eastern direction to a spot onshore where he could finally begin his journey *toward* Nineveh.

The story moves quickly for us, but that was not the case for Jonah. He would not begin walking toward Nineveh or hitching a ride in a caravan headed there anytime soon. Jonah would just need to stay in that fish's belly over the course of three days as the fish continued on its underwater journey.

Imagine Jonah already being in a dreadful state of mind as he entered what he expected to be his watery grave. That would be bad enough. But what was likely worse for him was that, instead of God letting him drown and die a relatively quick death, he faced the unexpected horror of being grabbed by the fish, sliding down its gullet, and splashing down into its belly.

Being swallowed whole by a big fish had to have been the most traumatic experience of Jonah's life. And there's no indication that he was the least bit unconscious during that terrible episode.

Jonah may not have been conscious during the entire three-day trip, but he was definitely conscious through part of it, because he prayed a prayer of repentance from within the fish's belly. And he remembered what he prayed so it could be recorded in what has become his amazing memoir.

No one has any idea how long it took Jonah to start praying to God, but it probably wouldn't take most of us very long if we were to deal with what Jonah went through. However, keep in mind that he had a bad attitude toward God (to be made clearer later), so his prayer of repentance may not have been immediate. Regardless of any speculation on timing, though, he did pray from within the belly of the fish.

Jonah called out to God from the deep.

Since Jonah was a prophet, he likely knew well the Scriptures available to him during his lifetime. Perhaps that can be seen in Jonah's prayer. There are similarities between David's words recorded in the book of Second Samuel and Jonah's statements. And it seems appropriate to compare the words in the prayer of Jonah to those of David.

David sang a song to the Lord after God "*rescued him from his enemies and from Saul*" (2 Samuel 22:1). Here is part of that song.

> *The waves of death overwhelmed me;*
> *floods of destruction swept over me.*

The grave wrapped its ropes around me;
death laid a trap in my path.
(2 Samuel 22:5–6)

David then called to the Lord.

But in my distress I cried out to the Lord*;*
yes, I cried to my God for help.
He heard me from his sanctuary;
my cry reached his ears.
(2 Samuel 22:7)

Then the Lord began taking action to deliver David from his trouble. Among other things David wrote to describe God's actions are,

Then at the command of the Lord*,*
at the blast of his breath,
the bottom of the sea could be seen,
and the foundations of the earth were laid bare.
He reached down from heaven and rescued me;
he drew me out of deep waters.
(2 Samuel 22:16–17)

Of course the *waves of death* that swirled around David were figurative, or symbolic—used to express his feelings of sinking toward destruction and drowning. And the *deep waters* out of which God drew David were also figurative. But such things were anything but figurative for Jonah. They were all too real.

Like David, Jonah called out to God in his distress; but as he did, real *waves of death* were indeed swirling around and overwhelming him. David looked to God in "His sanctuary"—where He dwells—and Jonah exalted God and abased himself when he looked to the Lord's *holy Temple* and cried out for mercy.

Then Jonah's prayer ascended to that holy Temple. God heard him from there and responded to his cry. He really did come down and draw Jonah out of *deep waters* when, after he spent three days in the fish's belly, the Lord delivered him from the watery pit he occupied.

From the deep, from the belly of the fish, Jonah prayed as he felt his life *slipping away*. Jonah called out to God for mercy. Then the Lord listened to his cry and responded to Jonah with both mercy and grace.

Jonah was a disobedient servant. He was a rebellious child of God, and he knew it. Jonah—the insubordinate preacher—knew exactly where he stood with the Creator at the time. He made a conscious effort to disobey his master. He knew the Lord caused the storm. And he acknowledged that it was actually God, not simply the sailors, who was responsible for hurling him into the deep (Jonah 2:3).

Sometimes it's awfully hard for people who consciously live in disobedience to God's will to come to a place of seeking forgiveness. Turning from disobedient ways can be difficult. And sometimes it's hard for people knowingly running from responsibility to repent and finally accept and do what's required of them. Even today, Jonah serves as an example to us of that.

Jonah was, in fact, a very hard case. Multitudes of people are brought to the place of repentance with much less trouble. It took extraordinary actions by God to bring Jonah there. And here is where we should become absolutely impressed with not only the extent of God's grace but also His pursuit of the lost and disobedient.

We don't have to wait until we read about God forgiving the people of Nineveh to be impressed with the magnitude of God's willingness to forgive sin.

If God had acted in Jonah's case in a way that most people would expect, Jonah's story would not have turned out the way it did. And to be honest, perhaps you and I could have been satisfied with a different ending.

If the story had developed differently, we could have satisfied ourselves with reading of God's justice being brought to bear against Jonah instead of His grace. We could have considered the Lord as being entirely justified if He saw to it that Jonah was immediately torn to shreds by sharks as soon as the pathetic, disobedient servant hit the water.

Truthfully, we most likely could have been content with a story about Jonah in which we were told he was eaten by a fish God brought up from the deep, and then the Lord called another preacher to do the job that Jonah wouldn't do. There still would have been plenty to learn from a story like that. But the lessons we could learn in that case would not be nearly as powerful as those God teaches us today through the book of Jonah.

God had every right to destroy Jonah for disobeying Him. But He cared enough not to do that. He cared not only about Jonah fulfilling his mission—his appointment by God—He cared *personally* about both him and his future.

The Lord had every right to allow him to sink to the bottom of the sea like a rock. He had every right to allow Jonah to be digested and expelled as excrement by any fish that happened to eat him—whole or otherwise. But that was not God's plan.

It was not God's plan for the disobedient man to be destroyed. It was God's plan for him to be delivered from not only the physical pit but also the spiritual pit he was in. It wasn't just Nineveh's future that God was concerned about; He was concerned about Jonah's future.

The Lord wanted to change his mind, and He was going about doing it. He was attentive to Jonah's most critical need, and meeting that need was so important to God that He went to extreme measures to do it.

It was God's plan for Jonah to repent of what he had done in disobeying the Lord. It was His plan to convince Jonah to stop running from Him and stop avoiding his responsibilities. And it was God's plan for Jonah to change his attitudes.

The Lord's plan and desire was not only for Jonah to carry a message of judgment and destruction to Nineveh but also for Jonah to cry out to Him to be saved from his own destruction.

God wanted to hear Jonah call out to Him in prayer, repent, and say, "*I will fulfill all my vows.*"

He wanted to show Jonah, and us, that God cares enough to listen and save.

CHAPTER 6

GOD CARES ENOUGH TO PROVIDE A SIGN

IN THIS CHAPTER we pause in our progress through the book of Jonah to consider an important part that Jonah's story still plays today in revealing God's overall plan to redeem us.

Many people don't consider the book of Jonah's place in the Bible to be all that important. And there are those who are so skeptical of its truth that they dismiss it entirely as fiction. (Not surprisingly, those skeptics also tend to be those who don't believe in the infallibility of Scripture.) But the book, its story, and the truths we glean from it are critically important.

One sure piece of evidence of the eternal importance of Old Testament Scriptures is how New Testament writers used and referred back to the words of the Old Testament. The Old Testament stood then, and still stands today, as the foundation used by God to establish our path to redemption and justification by faith.

When we see and understand that the same Holy Spirit who inspired the Old Testament writers also inspired New Testament writers to examine, teach, and include references to passages in the Old Testament in their writings, the truth and value of the Old Testament is firmly sealed. And before we go on, let's establish God's own personal, undeniable approval of the Old Testament. Then we'll see and understand the significance of something that many people miss.

And that is:

An important part of the understanding and confidence we place in the overarching theme of all Scripture —both Old and New Testaments—actually hinges on the truth and dependability of the book of Jonah.

Drive another stake down by this: Jesus himself taught that the Scriptures already accepted by the Jews in the days of His ministry were holy and inspired by God. I refer here to books in the *Septuagint,* the Greek LLX translation containing all 39 books that exist today in the Old Testament.

According to Christianity.com, "Jesus and the Apostles studied, memorized, used, quoted, and read most often from the Bible of their day, the Septuagint." And according to John Barnett, writing for Christianity.com, "When Jesus quotes the Old Testament in Matthew [Matthew being written primarily to convince the Jews that Jesus of Nazareth is indeed their promised Messiah], He uses the Hebrew text only 10% of the time, but the Greek LXX translation 90% of the time!"[15]

Jesus' own spoken words commended those books that appear in what we know today as the Old Testament as being true and authoritative. He told the crowds,

---

15 https://www.christianity.com/jesus/birth-of-jesus/genealogy-and-jewish-heritage/what-bible-did-jesus-use.html, August 25, 2010, accessed August 6, 2023.

> *Don't misunderstand why I have come. I did not come to abolish the law of Moses or the writings of the prophets. No, I came to accomplish their purpose. I tell you the truth, until heaven and earth disappear, not even the smallest detail of God's law will disappear until its purpose is achieved.* (Matthew 5:17–18)

Side note: Needless to say, heaven and earth have yet to disappear. That means "its purpose" is still in the process of being achieved today.

When speaking of "*the law of Moses,*" Jesus was speaking in a narrow sense of the laws and principles contained in the *Torah* (which word comes from the Hebrew word for "law"). That "Law" is contained in the first five books of the Old Testament.

When speaking of "*the writings of the prophets,*" Jesus was referring to the books of the prophets contained in the Hebrew Scriptures. And among them is the book of Jonah.

Then in verse eighteen He used the term "law" again (in "*not even the smallest detail of God's law will disappear until its purpose is achieved*"). But in context, He used the words "*God's law*" in a much broader sense—which is still often done today among Jews when they speak of the entire Word of God. In this sense, therefore, Jesus referred to the complete Jewish Canon of Scripture that contains the Torah, the books of the Prophets, and the other books of the Old Testament referred to in Judaism as *The Writings.*

Here is an important takeaway: During the Lord's days of ministry on earth, the Torah and the books of the Prophets, as well as The Writings, were already recognized as authoritative Scripture used by the Jewish people, including Jesus. And it was most certainly those books now included in the Old Testament that Jesus, at the age of twelve, discussed with the teachers and spiritual leaders in the Temple courts (Luke 2:41–52).[16]

When Jesus said He did not *"come to abolish the law of Moses or the writings of the prophets,"* He was confirming the truth, dependability, and enduring longevity of the Holy Scriptures they knew and studied at the time.

Now consider this: When Jesus spoke to the crowds that day, He stood before them as *God made flesh.* That means Jesus stood there as not only Creator but also the inspiration for the assembly of the entire Hebrew collection of Scriptures. And as *God in the flesh,* He became a teacher of those same Scriptures!

As the supreme teacher of the Bible, then, Jesus himself verbally acknowledged to them and claimed the books within the Bible are authoritative, from the Creator (*"God's law"*), trustworthy, and unchangeable. And because of that, God's approval of Scripture extends to the entire story in the book of Jonah. We can trust the story as written.

But there's even more to consider about how Jonah fits into this discussion.

I'm asking you for your patience as you begin reading the following section. I'll indeed address the importance of the book of Jonah when it comes to how the story it contains plays a critical role in the confidence we have in Scripture. But I'll

---

16 According to multiple sources, the Septuagint—that contained the Greek translation of the Hebrew Scriptures we have in the Old Testament today—was in common use at that time and was, of note, used by both Jesus and Paul. https://www.biblestudytools.com/bible-study/tips/what-bible-did-jesus-use-11638841.htm, accessed August 13, 2023.

take a little time setting the stage for it. In doing that, I base my comments on a narrative contained in Matthew chapter twelve.

Jesus was ministering in the towns of Galilee.[17] While doing so, He and His disciples were passing through a field of grain on a certain Sabbath day. As they passed through the field, His disciples plucked the heads of some of the grain because they were hungry (Matthew 12:1).

> *But some Pharisees saw them do it and protested, "Look, your disciples are breaking the law by harvesting grain on the Sabbath."* (Matthew 12:2)

In Jesus' response to the Pharisees (among the spiritual leaders of the day), He challenged their thinking on such things with His *words* (vv. 3–8) and continued on His way with His disciples. Then, He followed that by going to the synagogue of those same Pharisees, and there, He challenged them with His *actions.*

Jesus noticed a man there in the synagogue who had a deformed hand. Those same Pharisees knew Jesus healed the sick and lame everywhere He went, so they intentionally set a trap for Him as a challenge.

> *The Pharisees asked Jesus, "Does the law permit a person to work by healing on the Sabbath?" (They were hoping he would say yes, so they could bring charges against him.)*
>
> (Matthew 12:10b)

---

17 "When Jesus had finished giving instructions to His twelve disciples, He went on from there to teach and to preach in their [Galilean] cities" (Matthew 11:1 AMP).

Instead of accepting that Jesus had been sent by God, the Pharisees went about plotting to find a way to stop His ministry. But that was not going to keep Jesus from doing what He came to earth to do.

> *And he answered, "If you had a sheep that fell into a well on the Sabbath, wouldn't you work to pull it out? Of course you would. And how much more valuable is a person than a sheep! Yes, the law permits a person to do good on the Sabbath."*
>
> *Then he said to the man, "Hold out your hand." So the man held out his hand, and it was restored, just like the other one! Then the Pharisees called a meeting to plot how to kill Jesus.*
>
> (Matthew 12:11–14)

Imagine the hard hearts of those Pharisees as they believed maintaining their own status and positions was more important than bringing healing to those in need. Jesus continued ministering in the same way everywhere He went. And everywhere He went, the people followed.

Soon someone brought to Jesus a demon-possessed man who couldn't speak and was blind, and *"He healed the man so that he could both speak and see"* (v. 22b).

Those who witnessed that were amazed by such a miracle and asked, *"Could it be that Jesus is the Son of David, the Messiah?"* (v. 23). By saying that, the people were coming closer to accepting Jesus as their deliverer and savior sent by God.

> *But when the Pharisees heard about the miracle, they said, "No wonder he can cast out demons. He gets his power from Satan, the prince of demons."* (Matthew 12:24)

It was at that time when Jesus called the Pharisees a "brood of vipers."[18] He made it clear that their vicious words proved they had evil hearts, and they would be judged accordingly. But those Pharisees who continually kept up with Jesus' travels and ministry didn't change. And before long they tried to come up with another way to discredit Him.

> *One day some teachers of religious law and Pharisees came to Jesus and said, "Teacher, we want you to show us a miraculous sign to prove your authority."* (Matthew 12:38)

Those who opposed the Lord wanted to see a sign!

They had already decided to have Jesus killed—undoubtedly in order to keep Him from taking over the minds of the people, which was a threat to their positions and power. Then they made a pretense of being willing to accept the ministry of Christ if He would show them a sign.

They were filled with such hypocrisy! And Jesus knew their thoughts.

> *But Jesus replied, "Only an evil, adulterous generation would demand a miraculous sign; but the only sign I will give them is the sign of the prophet Jonah. For as Jonah was in the belly of the great fish for three days and three nights, so will the Son of Man be in the heart of the earth for three days and three nights.*
>
> *"The people of Nineveh will stand up against this generation on judgment day and condemn it, for they repented of their sins at the preaching of Jonah. Now someone greater than Jonah is here—but you refuse to repent. The queen of Sheba will also*

---

18 "Vipers" in the NKJV, "Brood of snakes" in the NLT (Matthew 12:34).

> *stand up against this generation on judgment day and condemn it, for she came from a distant land to hear the wisdom of Solomon. Now someone greater than Solomon is here—but you refuse to listen."* (Matthew 12:39–42)

Jesus compared His coming death and resurrection to Jonah's experience as written in the Old Testament. By doing so, with these words combined with His words we previously considered from Matthew chapter five verses 17 through 18, Jesus—God in the flesh, the Word made flesh, the One through whom all Creation was brought into being—confirmed the story of Jonah as **recorded truth**.

The result of this is that no one can legitimately refuse to believe what is written in the book of Jonah without also refusing to believe Jesus' own affirmation of it.

While discounted by many, the book of Jonah is extremely important. God uses Jonah's story to teach us many lessons, and among them is the truth about the death and resurrection of our Lord.

Then take note of this amazing fact:

A search of the Bible will reveal that outside of the book named for Jonah and the very short mention of him in 2 Kings 14:25—which I related to you at the beginning of this book—Jonah is mentioned in the Bible ***only*** **by Jesus**, and then only in the context of Jonah's experience pointing toward Jesus' identity as Messiah and His death and resurrection.

Disregard the book of Jonah at your own peril. Scoff at the idea of Jonah praying from the belly of the fish. Contend there's no way Jonah could have spent three days in the belly of the fish and lived to let others know about it; but the account is totally true. And if you can't believe it, then you can't believe the words of Jesus when He affirmed all of the Old Testament and spoke of Jonah to the Pharisees and teachers of the law.

Matthew and Luke were the only two New Testament writers to include what Jesus said about Jonah. Luke recorded in chapter eleven that Jesus also spoke of Jonah being a *sign* to the Ninevites (which also seals the accuracy of that part of Jonah's story). And in that passage of Scripture, Luke recorded Jesus telling the people that what they would see happening to Him—relative to that sign of Jonah—would also be a sign to them that *He was sent by God.*

> *As the crowd pressed in on Jesus, he said, "This evil generation keeps asking me to show them a miraculous sign. But the only sign I will give them is the sign of Jonah. What happened to him was a sign to the people of Nineveh that God had sent him. What happens to the Son of Man will be a sign to these people that he was sent by God."* (Luke 11:29–30)

The sign Jesus gave to them was later fulfilled before their very eyes. And through the words of Jesus himself, we—you and I today—can therefore be assured of the reality, accuracy, and importance of the narrative contained in the book of Jonah.

To the people of Nineveh, God's dealings with Jonah was a sign that He meant business. And then Jesus used the sign of Jonah to direct the attention of people—including us—to the powerful truth of His claims as their Messiah and our Savior.

We should come to understand and accept that God demonstrated His concern not only for the people of Nineveh but also for us by orchestrating His response to Jonah's disobedience. And to that end, the Lord provided to us the sign of Jonah to teach us not one, but two, very clear and important lessons:

(1) Just as God sent Jonah to the Ninevites, He sent Jesus to the Jews.

(2) Just as Jonah spent three days in the belly of a fish, Jesus spent three days in the heart of the earth.

The Word of God has proven itself time and time again to be true and dependable. You can place your confidence in Jonah's story. And you can be assured that the account of Christ's death and resurrection—that procured for us both our salvation and eternal hope—was not a fabrication of man's imagination.

God indeed cares enough to provide a sign.

CHAPTER 7

GOD CARES ENOUGH TO PERFORM MIRACLES

Then the L*ORD ordered the fish to spit Jonah out onto the beach.*
(Jonah 2:10)

WE CANNOT GO far into a study of Jonah before running into the controversy of whether or not Jonah actually died during his sojourn within the fish's belly. There are those who believe Jonah did die; in fact, they will say that he *had* to die in order for his experience to fully illustrate the death of Christ.

Much effort has been expended by those who want to convince others that they're right about Jonah dying and being raised from the dead when the fish vomited Jonah onto dry land. Some even claim that it was more than a fish's belly from which Jonah prayed. They claim he prayed from the grave, or the place of the dead, itself.

But the Bible doesn't support that. Scripture doesn't provide any of us hope that a person can repent and pray to God from the grave with the result of being saved or delivered after death. From a Scriptural standpoint, I'm of the opinion that idea is merely one of a number of teachings dredged up from a combination of wishful thinking and an earthbound understanding.[19]

Now is our opportunity to repent—now, as we live and have opportunity in this life—not later after we've died.

> *For God says, "At just the right time, I heard you. On the day of salvation, I helped you." Indeed, the "right time" is now. Today is the day of salvation.* (2 Corinthians 6:2)

But we don't need to merely rest on those words of Paul to settle the topic of limits placed on prayers of salvation or deliverance. Consider, too, that we actually have an account in the Bible that provides to us one imminent authority's special and personal insight into the land and positions of the dead. It was Jesus himself who directly and clearly addressed limitations on the movement of those who have died.

Jesus gave His disciples the account of Lazarus and the rich man (Luke 16:19–31). Lazarus, a very poor man when it comes to earth's possessions, died and went to be with Abraham—to an afterlife of peace and comfort. Then the rich man died and went to an afterlife of torment (vv. 22–23).

Many people talk of that story as simply being a parable—a good story with an important moral, and a story told using events that actually didn't happen in a truly historical sense. But regardless of any title (as in "The Parable of . . .") that Bible

---

19 When it comes to finding support for the idea of praying for salvation after we die and things such as "Purgatory" and prayers or offerings made for the sake of the dead, people look to and interpret writings known as *apocryphal* books—which are writings that were not included in the final, authorized Hebrew canon of Scripture. Some books of the Apocrypha have been included in Catholic and Orthodox Bibles while being rejected by the majority of other autonomous branches of Christianity.

translators, preachers, or Bible teachers may have given to the passage of Scripture containing Jesus' words about Lazarus and the rich man, Jesus did not tell that story as a parable.

Jesus taught by using parables, but in the Bible, there was no parable told by Jesus in which He named names. The story of Lazarus stands alone in that regard. Lazarus was a real person, and he really died. And since Lazarus was a real person, the rich man also was a real person, but Jesus saw no need to reveal his name. Some people have referred to the rich man by the name of Dives, but his name is not stated in Scripture.

Jesus revealed in His discourse that the rich man could look up in anguish from his place of torment and actually see Lazarus living in a place of comfort. He could also see the father of their nation, Abraham, who was there with Lazarus. Jesus also revealed the rich man could indeed pray, or call out, for help. But there was no hope given to him that his prayer, his request, could be answered with anything other than a NO.

> *The rich man shouted, "Father Abraham, have some pity! Send Lazarus over here to dip the tip of his finger in water and cool my tongue. I am in anguish in these flames."* (Luke 16:24)

Abraham was able to respond to the rich man, and he spoke words to him the rich man didn't want to hear—words a good many people today also don't want to believe.

> *But Abraham said to him, "Son, remember that during your lifetime you had everything you wanted, and Lazarus had nothing. So now he is here being comforted, and you are in anguish. And besides, there is a great chasm separating us. No one can cross over to you from here, and no one can cross over to us from there."* (Luke 16:25–26)

In Jesus' relation of that, He pictured for His listeners only two abodes that exist beyond the grave. One of them is a place of comfort. The other one is a place of anguish among tormenting flames. And three things about the afterlife were made clear in Abraham's response.

First, Abraham addressed what happened—or didn't happen—in the rich man's lifetime. The time we live from our natural birth to our death is the time in which we experience all that an earthly life affords us. It's where we walk, live, accumulate possessions, and learn about love, hate, and compassion. It's where we respond to God's commandments, His grace, and His calls to repent and begin living for Him.

Second, Abraham confirmed the eternal states of souls after death. After death we receive either comfort or anguish in the future contingent on the decisions we make in this life.

Third, Abraham made it clear that in the afterlife—existence after death—there is no way for someone who died to move from the place of anguish to the place of comfort, or vice versa. *No one can cross over* to the place of comfort from the place of anguish.

But there's even more.

> *Then the rich man said, "Please, Father Abraham, at least send him to my father's home. For I have five brothers, and I want him to warn them so they don't end up in this place of torment."*
>
> *But Abraham said, "Moses and the prophets have warned them. Your brothers can read what they wrote."* (Luke 16:27–29)

The conversation between the rich man and Abraham went on for a while, and the rich man argued and continued to appeal—or, pray, if you will.

> *The rich man replied, "No, Father Abraham! But if someone is sent to them from the dead, then they will repent of their sins and turn to God."*
>
> *But Abraham said, "If they won't listen to Moses and the prophets, they won't be persuaded even if someone rises from the dead."* (Luke 16:30–31)

In what Abraham said to the rich man, I believe there is a clear allusion to the future responses of people to Jesus after His resurrection.

Even today, plenty of people care nothing about what Moses and the prophets wrote—words giving us God's standards and words that foretold or projected the coming of the Messiah, our Savior. People today still reject the important messages in their writings; so like those who rejected Jesus in New Testament times because they didn't listen to Moses and the prophets, they too reject the Savior today—the One who indeed died and rose from the dead to save them.

But as we stay focused for a moment longer on Jesus' description of the events as they applied to the situation of the rich man, let's consider something else.

Besides being omnipresent (present everywhere) and omnipotent (all powerful), God is also omniscient (all knowing). So beyond doubt, God witnessed the conversation between Abraham and the rich man. Jesus, as God in the flesh, knew all the details about what He was telling them about the rich man and Lazarus.

Also, in what He revealed that day, it's evident that even the rich man knew he could not change his destiny. Although the rich man called out, he didn't pray to be delivered from the grave or the torment he was experiencing. He first prayed only for Lazarus to be sent to him to bring him some comfort. And when that was denied, he prayed that Abraham would send someone to warn his brothers not to come where he was.

The rich man knew the truth of his lasting position after death even before Abraham confirmed it.

Remember, these are the *red-letter* words of Jesus. These are not the teachings or interpretations of any other. These are not merely the understandings of someone who has been or is now a follower of Christ. And Jesus didn't go about leading people to believe fairy tales containing false hopes. Jesus gave us a clear revelation of truth concerning the finality of positions in the afterlife.

So regardless of where someone thinks Jonah might have gone after he died (relative to the views of those who believe that), he could not have changed his habitation as the result of a prayer made from the grave.

It would have been a great story if God had sent Jonah into the flames (where he possibly deserved to go) for three days to punish him and then delivered him so he could go to Nineveh after he cried out from there for forgiveness. But that's not in Jonah's story.

And taking that further, it seems to me that three days in hell would have drastically changed Jonah's heart. But we'll eventually find out later that his underlying problem God was dealing with all along was still there even after spending three days in the belly of the fish. It will become clear as we continue reading that while Jonah's ordeal with the fish convinced him to obey God and preach in Nineveh, it didn't fix his attitudes.

After seeing what can be learned from the story of Lazarus and the rich man as told by Jesus, we look at what Jonah himself said as recorded in Scripture. According to what is contained in the book of Jonah, he prayed while he was clearly alive and conscious.

As my life was slipping away,
I remembered the LORD.
And my earnest prayer went out to you
in your holy Temple.
(Jonah 2:7)

So for those who say Jonah actually died in the fish's belly and was resurrected when the fish spit him out on the beach, even if he did die, he certainly did *not* call out in repentance after he died. He did, however, certainly realize he was as good as dead at the time.

When Jonah said, *"I called to you from the land of the dead"* (Jonah 2:2), he had to have been speaking figuratively (in clear Davidic, poetic fashion); for after that, he said otherwise. He said *his earnest prayer* went out to God "***as*** [his] *life was slipping away*" (emphasis mine).

To say that he prayed from hell or the grave in more than a figurative sense cannot be supported by Scripture. I admit it makes some sense to my human mind that Jonah died—and maybe he did—for no one can explain fully in earthly terms how Jonah could actually stay alive in a fish's belly for so long. However, we have already spoken about God's power to do what He wants.

Nothing is beyond the Creator's ability. He could have raised Jonah from the dead, or He could have sustained his life in the belly of the fish for three days. Either one was miraculous. Truthfully, though, I don't believe it really matters one way or the other when gathering what God wants us to learn from the book of Jonah.

I actually see the controversy as a distraction even though I felt it's one I needed to address. For I don't see that Jesus attempted to convince anyone that Jonah died and was raised from the dead. So why should anyone else spend time doing it?

Jesus simply said that "*as Jonah was* ***in*** *the belly of the great fish for three days and three nights, so will the Son of Man be* ***in*** *the heart of the earth for three days and three nights*" (Matthew 12:40 [emphasis mine]).

We know Jesus died, but whether or not Jonah died (or needed to die for Scripture to be fulfilled) is not clear at all; neither is it addressed. That's mere opinion, not Scriptural fact. Jonah's death happening while in the belly of the fish and his resurrection happening when the fish spit him out on the beach is purely a matter for speculation.

It changes nothing of the truly important things that can be gleaned from the book of Jonah.

If we aren't careful—if we don't remain balanced in our pursuit of truth—we can find ourselves getting sidetracked onto a tangent, away from what God wants us to learn. In our attempts to satisfy our human minds, we can get so involved with trying to explain everything in the Bible that challenges our understanding that we're led astray.

It's possible for us to get so caught up in needing to understand everything, or in needing to find meaningful symbology in every minor thing we can think of, that we overlook the importance of what God is revealing to us in Scripture. And that can lead us toward diminishing or departing from the simple faith that's required for believing God.

What I'm saying may leave you with the impression that I'm opposed to theological study and the pursuit of understanding. But I'm not. I'm interested in theology. However, I do feel strongly that theological scholarship should never be allowed to become an end in itself.

The need to satisfy ourselves by finding natural or scientific explanations for everything we read in the Bible, or the need to continually dig out hidden secrets through theological pursuits until everything satisfies the human mind, is not required of us.

We are told to study to show ourselves approved of God (2 Timothy 2:15 KJV). But there is no commandment in the Bible ordering us to spend our entire lives and all our energy figuring out every intricate detail of the secrets of God.

Sometimes we need to remind ourselves that as long as people can read and understand the words of the Bible, Scripture has the ability to speak to their hearts without the assistance of anyone else and without them pursuing high levels of formal education.

People with high levels of education in spiritual things can certainly help us. Thank God for those called and led by the Holy Spirit to study, preach, reveal, and teach us the truth of God's Word. But the Holy Spirit also has the ability to do just fine on His own in speaking personally one-on-one with people. In fact, the Holy Spirit can speak directly through the Word of God and enlighten minds and hearts in ways that no one else will ever be able to do through his or her own efforts.

Also, besides that, regardless of how long we study, dig, and try to understand all the mysteries of life and the Scriptures, none of us will come to a perfect knowledge of everything. There will always be things that only God knows; and ultimately, we all live by faith and trust our creator to know and understand all the things we don't.

We should study, search out, and lay hold of the truth of God's Word. But sometimes if penchants toward academic pursuits for the purpose of satisfying our earthly minds are not controlled, it can lead to even the most well-meaning people finding themselves having difficulty maintaining faith in what the Bible says.

Even as we go about harvesting truths from Scripture through our study of the book of Jonah, if we become wrapped up and overcome in our attempts to satisfy the understanding and interests of the flesh (which is never satisfied), we ourselves will have entered deep waters. And we must beware of the consequences of such a thing lest we become swallowed up by unbelief instead of by a big fish!

Bear with me if I'm somewhat repetitive with what I've already written, but I must get this across:

Cannot the Creator, who made the world and set the stars in space, make a fish—a one-of-a-kind specimen—for the sole purpose of swallowing Jonah?

Cannot the God who brought water out of the rock and gave the Israelites manna to eat supply Jonah with air to breathe during his sojourn in the fish's belly?

Cannot the One who walked with the three Hebrew children in the fire keep the caustic acid in the fish's stomach from digesting the disobedient man of God?

Perhaps Jonah died, and perhaps God raised him from the dead. God can do that! But perhaps Jonah was alive the whole time. If alive, perhaps he was conscious for much of that time. Perhaps he was unconscious. Perhaps he only prayed once soon after arriving in the fish's belly. Perhaps he prayed many times—even after he first felt his life *slipping away*.

But in the final analysis, what difference does it make? Does it change the message of the book of Jonah? Does it affect the lessons we learn from God's dealings with Jonah and the Ninevites? Clearly, if we allow an argument over whether or not Jonah died while in the fish to interfere with what is most important for us to learn from the book of Jonah, we're missing the point.

We should never permit ourselves to get so wrapped up in promoting our thoughts and opinions that they're allowed to take any focus off of what Scripture plainly reveals. Without apology, I admonish anyone who reads this to never allow satisfying your curiosity about things hidden from you become such a priority that your pursuit of gratifying the human mind complicates or obscures in any way what the Bible openly and forthrightly makes known.

Regardless of whether Jonah died or lived in the belly of the fish, the entire story of Jonah is filled with miraculous events. The entire story of Jonah is true and a miracle itself. And contained within its words is a miraculous revelation of God's patience, grace, mercy, and desire to save.

We must not allow that to be overshadowed, missed, or minimized in any way.

God cares enough to perform miracles, and there's more—much more—to come as we continue to learn from the book of Jonah!

CHAPTER 8

GOD CARES ENOUGH TO CALL AGAIN

> *Then the* Lord *spoke to Jonah a second time: "Get up and go to the great city of Nineveh, and deliver the message I have given you."* (Jonah 3:1–2)

WE'RE NOT TOLD where the fish spit out Jonah. We can only surmise the fish swam with him in its belly to somewhere on the eastern shore of the Mediterranean. Regardless, though, it was surely a place chosen by God—a place from where Jonah would finally be able to begin a journey *toward* Nineveh.

To stand on the shore enjoying the scenery and suddenly see a giant fish swim up close to the shore and spit a man out of its mouth would be quite impressive—and shocking. What a sight it must have been for any fishermen who might have been close by mending their nets that day!

I can imagine that Jonah perhaps lay motionless on the ground for quite a while; we don't know. But the fish's work was done, and after depositing its cargo onto dry land, the fish no doubt turned and swam back out to deep waters, leaving

Jonah behind to gather his senses and recover from being within the close confines of the fish's belly.

We're not told about anyone finding Jonah on the beach and nursing him back to health. That could have happened. But in my mind, after imagining him somewhat reviving from his ordeal, I visualize him walking or dragging himself back into the ocean to bathe in the salt water in an attempt to get the stench of the fish off of him—along with any residue from the fish's stomach that coated his skin.

Just the thought of that is sickening.

Many details we would like to know about the events are left out of the story. For one, we are given no information about how long it took for Jonah to recover from his terrible experience or what that process involved.

The writer of the story spends time revealing to us only the most important things—what he wanted us to know. And for sure, we're told that sometime after Jonah was delivered from the belly of the fish (which, again, according to Jesus foreshadowed His own resurrection), the Lord spoke to him a second time.

It's an important thing when God speaks. Nothing He says should be taken lightly. The Lord has the right to speak to us and give us any directions He chooses, and He has the right to be relentless in His communications and demands. The Creator is all powerful, and He was teaching Jonah that no one has the right to oppose Him or ignore His will when He speaks.

God spoke to Jonah again, and once again He told him to go to Nineveh and proclaim to its citizens the message He gave him to deliver.

God showed himself to be forgiving and willing to give His disobedient servant a second chance. And Jonah responded by finally making his way toward Nineveh.

As Christians, we should be well-acquainted with God's grace, and we should understand that Jonah was experiencing a large measure of it. We know the Lord is full of mercy. He forgives us when we confess our failures, so we really shouldn't be surprised by God being willing to forgive Jonah.

Christians carry a message of restoration, and that message is demonstrated in the book of Jonah. But we need to move forward in humility with this thought, too, for God's willingness to show us mercy is *His* choice. There comes a time when the Lord's mercy ends and His justice begins, but we're shown in the book of Jonah that it's definitely up to God to determine the timing.

Ultimately, God does not owe us opportunity after opportunity to repent and do His will. But He often allows people multiple chances to get things right, and that's clearly demonstrated in the story of Jonah.

As I've already mentioned in another way, God would have been justified in ridding the world of such a disobedient servant, but the Lord didn't do that. He instead performed miracles to bring Jonah to repentance, and then He continued to work miraculously on Jonah's behalf after he cried out to Him from the fish's belly.

The Lord demonstrated in amazing and convincing ways that He was not going to give up on Jonah. Even Jonah's significant disobedience and failure didn't disqualify him from hearing God call out to him again. It also didn't disqualify Jonah from going about fulfilling the mission the Lord gave him. God forgave and saved the life of that preacher when he repented. Then He repeated His call.

This is notable: the Lord did **not** withdraw *His original call* from Jonah because of his disobedience. His will for Jonah—and Jonah's mission—remained the same.

God had not changed His mind. Once again He called out to Jonah and told him to go to Nineveh. Then it was left up to Jonah to stand true to his word. He told God while imprisoned within the fish, *"I will fulfill all my vows"* (Jonah 2:9b), and it was time for him to do it.

The Apostle Paul wrote in the book of Romans about the dynamics of Gentiles being brought into the Church. He wanted both Gentiles and Jews alike to understand the establishment of the healthy Body of Christ and the spiritual elements within it. Paul likened Jews who had rejected the gospel to branches that had been broken off a tree. And he likened Gentiles to branches that had been grafted into the same tree.

In giving them that illustration, Paul wanted the Gentile believers to understand that God had not forever rejected the Jews because they were rejecting Him. Paul let them know that just as God allowed Gentiles who were originally not part of the tree to *become* part of the tree (grafted into it), God would certainly allow unbelieving Jews to be grafted back into the tree if they repented of their unbelief (Romans 11:17–24).

During Paul's teaching on the topic, he made the point that God does not change His mind when it comes to fulfilling His redemptive plan. When He called out to His people to believe and follow Him in obedience, He did it forever. His call was not withdrawn because of their disobedience (even though their disobedience had consequences).

Paul wrote:

> *Many of the people of Israel are now enemies of the Good News, and this benefits you Gentiles. Yet they are still the people he loves because he chose their ancestors Abraham, Isaac, and Jacob. For God's gifts and his call can never be withdrawn.*
>
> (Romans 11:28–29)[20]

God called Jonah to preach for Him in Nineveh. The preacher refused to go. But that didn't change God's mind about what needed to be done. Plan A of the Lord's design was to call Jonah to do His will. And if Jonah had done that at the Creator's first call to him, his task of preaching God's message to the Ninevites could have been accomplished without all the delay and trouble he went through.

Plan A was not successful. So God turned to Plan B. And what was that plan? God's Plan B was for Jonah to simply go back to Plan A and start over.

We're shown in the story of Jonah that God cares enough to preserve our lives and include us in His plans—even when we're disobedient. And when we read about the Lord speaking to Jonah the second time, we're shown clearly that God cares enough to call again.

---

20 "Concerning the gospel they are enemies for your sake, but concerning the election they are beloved for the sake of the fathers. For the gifts and the calling of God are irrevocable" (Romans 11:28-29 NKJV).

CHAPTER 9

GOD CARES ENOUGH TO FORGIVE

> *This time Jonah obeyed the* Lord's *command and went to Nineveh, a city so large that it took three days to see it all. On the day Jonah entered the city, he shouted to the crowds: "Forty days from now Nineveh will be destroyed!"* (Jonah 3:3–4)

JONAH LEARNED HIS lesson. He honored his oath and did what the Lord called him to do. He went to the city of Nineveh and preached to its inhabitants.

The New King James Version of the Bible reads, "*Now Nineveh was an exceedingly great city, a three-day journey in extent.*" Nineveh was indeed a *great city*—the very large and populous city that later became the capital of the Assyrian Empire. If Jonah actually spent three days walking through and preaching in the city, it's interesting (but definitely not critical to the message of the book of Jonah) that three days is the same duration of time he spent inside the *great fish.*

Up to now we haven't known the message God wanted Jonah to preach to the Ninevites. But the Bible tells us that as soon as Jonah started his journey through Nineveh, he began preaching the message the Lord gave to him. And it was a simple one.

As translated in the New Living Translation of the Bible, it consisted of only eight words. And it seems Jonah cried out and repeated those same eight words over and over as he walked through the city.

"Forty days from now Nineveh will be destroyed!"

"Forty days from now Nineveh will be destroyed!"

"Forty days from now Nineveh will be destroyed!"

The contents of the book of Jonah lead us to believe he might have said nothing else. It's not recorded that Jonah had any conversations with anyone, and we read nothing in his story that requires us to believe that he had to have given anyone an explanation for why he was preaching that message. In fact, we'll find out from continuing our study that there are reasons why Jonah might have purposely avoided getting into conversations with the citizens of Nineveh.

It's reasonable to think, though, that people in Nineveh would have talked to Jonah and asked him about his message. And realizing that he could have been forever marked in his skin by the gastric fluids of the fish during his ordeal of being in the fish's belly for three days, it's also reasonable to think that people would have asked about what happened to him.

If Jonah did tell them about his ordeal, perhaps he told them what led to it. Maybe he told them how he didn't want to preach to them, that he ran from God, and that he was only fulfilling his responsibility to them because of what God did to him. Perhaps he told them the whole story, and that caused the people to take to heart the message he had for them.

But knowing Jonah's attitude toward the Ninevites (more to be said about that later), it's also possible that Jonah would not have even answered someone who asked him for details.

Jonah walked on and on throughout the city, shouting over and over again,

"Forty days from now Nineveh will be destroyed!"

"Forty days from now Nineveh will be destroyed!"

"Forty days from now Nineveh will be destroyed!"

There is nothing in the narrative of the book of Jonah itself to indicate specifics about why God was so angry with Nineveh. So we'll spend some time looking into that now to allow us to put God's message to the Assyrians in context. This will also increase our understanding of the preacher's reluctance to go to Nineveh.

Jonah was a prophet of *Israel.* Israel at that time was identified as the northern ten tribes of the twelve tribes of Israel—the twelve families that came from the sons of Jacob. From soon after the reign of Solomon, Israel existed as a separate nation apart from the nation of Judah to the south (that was made up of the two tribes of Judah and Benjamin).

Nineveh was part of the great Assyrian empire, and the Assyrians were the greatest threat to the Kingdom of Israel's existence for many years. The Assyrians were the dominant force in the Middle East at that time. They were warlike and harsh in the treatment of their enemies, and they caused the people of Israel much trouble for a very long time.

Israel, along with Syria and several other nations, had been brought into the sphere of the Assyrians' influence, and by the time Jonah was called to carry God's message to Nineveh, Israel had been forced to pay tribute to them for generations.

During the reign of Jeroboam II, king of Israel, and during the days of the ministry of Jonah, Israel began enjoying somewhat of a resurgence of autonomy that even resulted in the reinstatement of its rule over parts of its historical, geographic kingdom. As stated before, Jeroboam's success in leading Israel during that period of restoration was predicted by Jonah as recorded in 2 Kings 14:23–25.

But the Assyrians were extremely evil in dealing with the nations they conquered. They did all they could to strike terror into the minds of their enemies. They castrated men. They cut off the heads of their opposition and piled them up in towers as monuments to their cruelty. They captured and flayed their enemies. They skinned their opposition and displayed their skins draped over walls as testimonies to their ruthlessness.

They burnt their enemies' children. They impaled their victims on stakes and hung their heads from trees. They gouged out their eyes. They cut off hands, feet, noses, ears, and other parts of their enemies' bodies just to torture, terrify, and intimidate people. A simple search through the internet with the words "Assyrian depravity" will yield that and more.

The Assyrians were hated by other nations, especially those who were at their mercy. But they were not only masters of depravity in the treatment of their enemies; they were also ruthless expansionists, and I'm sure Jonah knew they were not going to go away, never to bother Israel again.

While Jonah knew God was giving his beloved nation a time of relative rest from foreign destroyers, he also knew that Jeroboam II was a man whose deeds were evil in the Lord's sight. And Jonah had to have considered that the nation of Israel was not experiencing the revival required to keep God from bringing their enemies back upon them even more violently than before as judgment for their sins.

Throughout the Old Testament we read about God using His people's enemies to chastise and bring judgment upon them when they didn't follow Him. But we also read that just as God judged His own people by using other nations—sometimes very evil ones—as His tools of justice, He also eventually judged those nations He allowed to punish His people when He determined the time was right.

For the Assyrians in Nineveh, their time of judgment had come. The Creator judged them, pronounced them guilty, and sentenced them to destruction for all their evil deeds—deeds that included their terrible mistreatment of Israel and its citizens.

God selected Jonah and sent him to declare to the Assyrians that their time of unbridled prosperity and influence was up. But according to the book of Jonah, his message of God's imminent judgment got through to the people in Nineveh and shook the city. Jonah's warning registered with them, and they not only came to believe it but also took immediate action.

> *The people of Nineveh believed God's message, and from the greatest to the least, they declared a fast and put on burlap to show their sorrow.* (Jonah 3:5)

Jonah's message and presence in Nineveh affected the entire city. In fact, his message even made it to the king, who also reacted to it with a sense of terror.

After hearing Jonah's message, the king didn't react as one would expect he would considering the mercilessness and arrogance of the Assyrians and their rulers. He didn't send soldiers to do away with Jonah or shut him up. Instead, the king rose from his throne, clothed himself with sackcloth, and sat down on a heap of ashes as a sign of sorrow and repentance (v. 6).

> *Then the king and his nobles sent this decree throughout the city:*
>
> *"No one, not even the animals from your herds and flocks, may eat or drink anything at all. People and animals alike must wear garments of mourning, and everyone must pray earnestly to God. They must turn from their evil ways and stop all their violence."* (Jonah 3:7–8)

The king, the one person you would never expect to yield to a mere prophet from Israel, also believed Jonah's message. The Assyrian king proclaimed a fast throughout the city. And of note, he included not only his human subjects in the fast but also all their animals.

Not only the citizens of Nineveh but also their animals were ordered to fast and be covered with sackcloth—a sign of contrition. But of even greater significance, the people were also commanded to pray to Jonah's God and give up their *"evil ways and stop all their violence."* They were told to call out to God for mercy and show the Lord they were serious about changing their ways.

Then pay close attention to what the king said to end his proclamation.

> *"Who can tell? Perhaps even yet God will change his mind and hold back his fierce anger from destroying us."* (Jonah 3:9)

The king and his subjects practiced true repentance, and it was done without any guarantee of success. The king may as well have said, "You never know, we might be able to get God to change His mind and give us a break!" It seems the king had no assurance from Jonah, or anyone else on earth, that their efforts to procure God's grace would work.

From the king's words we find our first evidence that Jonah did *not* give the Ninevites any hope of avoiding destruction at the hands of God. In other words, at this stage in the story we have no confidence at all that Jonah followed his warning with a call to repentance. And as we go on with our study, I believe that will be established.

The narrative in the rest of the book of Jonah causes me to believe adamantly that Jonah spent all of his time in Nineveh telling the people only that God was going to destroy them. In other words, Jonah didn't preach to the Ninevites a message that included hope for their future. Jonah's story encourages us to believe that he did *not* tell them God would forgive them if they repented of their sins.

Jonah did ***not*** give the people of Nineveh an altar call!

But something was working within the hearts of the people who heard Jonah's warning, and that prompted them to call out to God for mercy.

And since the king also became fully convinced there was only one solution to their dilemma—repentance—something powerful had to have been moving among the king's own thoughts for him to call his nation to repentance in order to see ***if*** God would forgive and not destroy them.

To me, there is only one convincing explanation for what caused the people to have any hope that God would relent and allow them to live. The king and the citizens of Nineveh had to have been moved to repentance by a special work of the Holy Spirit. The Spirit of God alone, not Jonah, had to have provided to them their only reason to hope.

Even if they had come to know Jonah's story, in Jonah's experience with the fish they would have found only a reason to accept the seriousness of God's words. But as the king began considering the facts (whatever the king knew), I believe the Holy Spirit must have helped him understand there had to be an underlying reason for God to go to such great lengths to have Jonah warn them.

The king must have considered that within God's warning there also existed a glimmer of hope, or there was no reason for the Lord to warn them of their pending destruction.

Thankfully for the Assyrians, even if there was only a thread of hope for them to cling to, that thread was enough for them as they developed their response to God in true repentance.

It was, indeed, enough; for,

> *When God saw what they had done and how they had put a stop to their evil ways, he changed his mind and did not carry out the destruction he had threatened.* (Jonah 3:10)

God did, in fact, relent from His plan to destroy them; and we learn a huge, important lesson through their experience.

God cares enough to forgive.

CHAPTER 10

GOD CARES ENOUGH FOR OUR ENEMIES

This change of plans greatly upset Jonah, and he became very angry. So he complained to the L*ORD* *about it: "Didn't I say before I left home that you would do this,* L*ORD*? *That is why I ran away to Tarshish! I knew that you are a merciful and compassionate God, slow to get angry and filled with unfailing love. You are eager to turn back from destroying people. Just kill me now,* L*ORD*! *I'd rather be dead than alive if what I predicted will not happen."* (Jonah 4:1–3)

AS WE BEGIN reading chapter four, the focus in Jonah's story shifts. He completed his duty to preach in Nineveh. And after he finished delivering his message to the Assyrians, it took no time at all for Jonah to switch from obediently delivering God's declaration of judgment to complaining to the Lord about His mercy.

Take note that Jonah expressed his frustration about it to the Lord *before* God actually proved He forgave the Ninevites and turned from His wrath—with that proof really coming only at the end of the forty days when God didn't destroy them.

It's apparent to me that the statement in verse ten of chapter three was interjected by the writer in hindsight, with knowledge of how the entire story of Jonah ended. And that's because it was *after* Jonah's complaint quoted above in verses one through three of chapter four when he went outside the city and sat down east of Nineveh to see what God's final response was going to be.

> *Then Jonah went out to the east side of the city and made a shelter to sit under as he waited to see what would happen to the city.* (Jonah 4:5)

After Jonah finished delivering his message of judgment, we don't read that God spoke to him and told him that He decided to forgive the Ninevites. And Jonah definitely didn't wait forty days for God's final answer before expressing his frustration to Him. So as I see it, all it took for Jonah to get upset was the mere *anticipation* of God honoring the Ninevites' fast and relenting of His plan to destroy Nineveh.

Jonah didn't need to wait for God to prove His forgiveness before getting upset. It seems clear to me that all Jonah actually needed to set him off emotionally was to see the people of Nineveh *begin* to repent. And surely, when the king himself began repenting and proclaimed a fast throughout the city, Jonah knew God's forgiveness of Nineveh was most likely a sealed deal.

Now we come to understand why Jonah attempted to run from the Lord the first time He called. And Jonah even admitted it openly. Basically (and this will sound strange), Jonah's motivation for deciding to run away and reject his calling was rooted in his own thorough knowledge of God. He was moved to run away from the Lord because he knew God!

He knew God very well.

Jonah wasn't pleased to see the people of Nineveh repent, and Jonah didn't need to wait until he saw God's final response to the Ninevites before getting angry. He was a preacher who wasn't glad to see the people respond to his message. He wasn't happy to hear that their leader had proclaimed a fast. In fact, I'm sure he was absolutely beside himself when he heard or read the king's proclamation.

Jonah had to have been especially frustrated by the king's words to his people: "*Who can tell? Perhaps even yet God will change his mind and hold back his fierce anger from destroying us.*"

It probably didn't physically happen, but in my imagination I hear Jonah's inward cry even if it wasn't audibly expressed. In my mind I see Jonah standing by himself in the middle of Nineveh with a look of total desperation and frustration. I see him throw his hands up and hear him say aloud in today's vernacular, "**Are you kidding me**? **Even the king**!"

Jonah's personal world was falling apart because the King of Assyria was catching on to what Jonah already knew. He made a conscious decision to run away from God because he knew preaching God's message to the Assyrians gave them the opportunity to repent.

And he did not want them to repent!

Jonah—God's very own prophet, His representative—didn't want the Assyrians to experience God's grace and forgiveness; he wanted them destroyed!

"Didn't I say before I left home that you would do this, Lord? That is why I ran away to Tarshish!"

No doubt Jonah loved trying to turn the hearts of the citizens of Israel back to the Lord, but he clearly had no passion at all for delivering God's words to Israel's enemies. By evaluating Jonah's response to both God's call to him and the repentance of the people in Nineveh, we can see that Jonah was much more nationalistic than evangelistic in his views. And he was especially not evangelistic toward his enemies.

The Assyrians were the epitome of evil. They were the enemies of God's people, and I'm sure because of that, Jonah felt strongly that they were God's enemies too. So in his mind, the only thing the Ninevites deserved was annihilation. Even though Jonah surely knew the Israelites had far to go before they pleased the Lord, he no doubt considered them worthy of God's patience—but not so for the Assyrians.

Jonah was not in favor of the Assyrians being saved in any way. Their salvation from destruction could result in Assyria having an opportunity to renew and increase even more their cruel domination over the Israelites. The prospect of that was without doubt something that he saw as intolerable.

I'm sure he was happy to have God use him to prophesy the positive things that Jeroboam would accomplish as king. And one would think he would have been even happier to be able to preach to the Assyrians to foretell the destruction of Nineveh. But he wanted no part in it. And that wasn't because he didn't revel in the thought of Nineveh being destroyed. Again, it was because he knew God!

Jonah knew the foundations of God's actions and warnings of judgment are built primarily of redemptive material. He knew the Lord is *eager to turn back from destroying people.*

Jonah didn't want the Ninevites to be redeemed. He wanted them smashed. He wasn't interested in preaching any message to Nineveh that the Holy Spirit could use to bring the Assyrians to repentance. He didn't want to fill the altars with repentant Assyrians seeking God. He wanted them banished from the earth!

From reading Jonah's complaint, we now know he had an unpleasant exchange with the Lord when he *was still at home.* Before he went to Joppa to find a ship going anywhere but in the direction of Nineveh, he actually had words with God about being called to preach there.

We now know Jonah actually acknowledged and was bold enough to tell God the reason he was running away from his calling—away from his responsibility to God. Sensing such strong feelings on Jonah's part about the mission God appointed him to undertake, I can envision Jonah arguing with God and having said something like this:

> Lord, I don't want to go to Nineveh. I agree you should judge and destroy them. They deserve to be judged and wiped off the face of the earth for the way they've treated your people. But it's not right for you to ask me to go there! Lord, you know very well that if I let them know you're going to move against them, it gives them an opportunity to respond to you by asking for your mercy. Lord, I don't want any part in that!

But Jonah's response to the Lord was even more serious. He didn't merely tell God that he didn't *want* to do it; through his actions he revealed that he *wouldn't* do it. And although he eventually went to Nineveh and preached the Lord's message to them after his experience with the great fish, it's clear that his attitude was still unchanged even after preaching in the city.

Even after all Jonah went through, he boldly complained to the Creator about His grace and mercy. It took no more than the possibility and a foreboding dread of God showing mercy for Israel's enemies—or perhaps we should say Jonah's enemies—to cause Jonah to complain openly to God and go into such a state of depression and rage that he asked God to kill him.

> *"Just kill me now, Lord! I'd rather be dead than alive if what I predicted will not happen,"* said Jonah.

We do well to consider how a man in Jonah's position could be so motivated as to wish he were dead over his disappointment that God was not going to destroy someone.

I suppose we could say Jonah was throwing himself a *whale* of a pity party. (That may be humorous, but sadly, it's true.) Imagine his attitude! He pouted and actually openly conceded to God that he was more concerned about his prediction of judgment failing than the entire population of Nineveh being brought to dust.

I believe everyone who reads this section should read it again and again. Let it sink deep into your heart. Let it bring you to tears, because Jonah is not the only individual who has lived, or is living today, who has developed such a selfish, ungodly, hateful, and spiritually-self-destructive attitude.

The Ninevites were facing God destroying them, and Jonah was moved to anger by his own feelings of disappointment about the prospect of God not doing it.

Poor Jonah. Boil down Jonah's thoughts, and they amount to something like,

> Oh no! This is terrible. This is tragic! The people of Nineveh are repenting, and I know God will forgive them. That infuriates me! I'm so upset and embarrassed by it all that I want to die!

He wasn't just angry about what was happening, though; it seems clear to me that he was also angry with God for *allowing* it to happen. After all, God had a hand in everything that happened after He called Jonah to go to Nineveh. It was God's message that Jonah had to preach. And God had everything to do with bringing the Ninevites to their knees in repentance.

It was all God's doing!

I imagine Jonah thinking, "How could God allow such injustice?"

As for the Assyrians, he may have thought,

> How could God let them get away with gaining His mercy? After all they've done, what right do they have to call out to God? What right do they have to experience God's grace?
>
> What's fair about this? Why did God include me in this? I didn't ask for it! This isn't what I signed up for. What have I done to deserve to be humiliated like this?

Aha! We have come to the very reason God called Jonah in the first place. The people of Nineveh weren't the only ones who needed to wake up to reality. There were others, and one of them was definitely a preacher named Jonah.

But that's not all. Since God's dealings with Jonah are written in the Bible, and since we're reading it, He also wants *us* to face the same reality. God wants us to realize *beyond a shadow of doubt* that God cares enough—even for our enemies.

CHAPTER 11

GOD CARES ENOUGH TO TALK TO US

The L*ORD replied, "Is it right for you to be angry about this?"*
(Jonah 4:4)

THE NARRATIVE IN the book of Jonah is captivating from beginning to end, but it has now entered a dramatic phase. It has come to the point where the focus of the narrative swings even more directly onto Jonah's attitudes and his own relationship with God. The spotlight sharpens as the Lord confronts Jonah's complaint and speaks directly to him about his anger.

Jonah's feelings have been more fully revealed to us now, and it's time for us to learn even more about *God's* feelings. Understanding the actions and attitudes of both parties is important for our ability to learn the lessons the Lord wants to teach us through the story of Jonah, his ministry in Nineveh, and God's responses to not only the Assyrians but also Jonah.

It's incumbent upon us—entirely necessary—to do everything we can to understand the viewpoints of both the Lord and the preacher who attempted to run from Him.

Now getting to God's response to Jonah's complaint—the first question God asked him—it appears that Jonah didn't give the Lord an answer. Instead, it seems that he just shut his mouth and left Nineveh to wait outside the city to see what God would do next. (I'm repeating, below, the verse I included early in the previous chapter.)

> *Then Jonah went out to the east side of the city and made a shelter to sit under as he waited to see what would happen to the city.* (Jonah 4:5)

I'm just assuming that it took three days for Jonah to work his way through the city. If true, it's possible that was all the time that passed between when Jonah first began proclaiming God's word to the Ninevites and when he went outside the city to wait. So if Jonah wanted to wait at a distance but in sight of the city of Nineveh, to see what would happen to it, he had to be willing to wait for quite a while.

From the information we have in Jonah's story, it's reasonable to assume the Ninevites could not have known if their prayers and fasting moved God to turn from His judgment of them until at least forty days following the day Jonah began preaching. (Jonah certainly wouldn't have told them God was going to forgive them.) And when Jonah went outside the city to wait, he also needed to give God thirty-seven to forty days to reveal to him His final decision on the future of Nineveh—to see if the Lord would at all honor his complaint.

Beyond doubt, it doesn't take over a month for God to decide how to deal with anyone's response to His directions and warnings. God already knew how He was going to handle Nineveh, just as He already knew how He was going to handle

Jonah—the disobedient preacher with the attitude. But Jonah knew he had to wait.

Jonah knew he had no right to demand that God move any sooner than He had committed himself to move in order to reveal to both the people of Nineveh and Jonah that He indeed turned from His wrath toward the Assyrians (despite Jonah's temper tantrum). And after what we've already read, it seems like the height of arrogance for Jonah to even appear to challenge God.

Surely it was unreasonable for Jonah to expect the Creator to respond to his complaint of injustice by being anything more than what Jonah already knew and confessed Him to be. He knew God commonly responded to repentance with forgiveness. But still, Jonah waited.

Could it be that Jonah thought his arguments were so convincing that God should feel challenged by them? Maybe? I have only questions about that. Regardless of Jonah's reasoning, though, he did in fact wait to see what God would do. And in order to be able to protect himself in the environment outside of Nineveh while he waited, he built a shelter.

It seems that Jonah was prepared to wait to the end of the entire forty-day period. We don't know, however, if he actually ended up doing that. But he evidently did wait there in his shelter for at least some period of time as day after day he attempted to avoid the harshness of the environment.

One can only wonder about Jonah's state of mind throughout the whole period of his sojourn there outside of Nineveh. I'm sure it wasn't peaceful and calm. Perhaps he and God continued to have several conversations as Jonah waited—perhaps not. We can't know. But one thing we do know is that the Lord had started a conversation with Jonah, and by reading ahead we know it was sure to continue.

There were still things to discuss. There were still some feelings to straighten out. We'll soon read that God wasn't done with Jonah. He continued to personally and deliberately affect circumstances in Jonah's life in His attempt to change him and give him the new heart he desperately needed to receive.

We'll read that the Lord followed up His first question to Jonah by speaking clearly to him again, and it too was recorded to further our own knowledge of God and His involvement in His Creation—His activities in our lives and the world around us.

However, we have already been introduced to the compelling fact that when a problem is brewing in our hearts and minds, regardless of our status in His kingdom, God cares enough to talk to us about it.

CHAPTER 12

GOD CARES ENOUGH TO SEND A WORM

And the LORD God arranged for a leafy plant to grow there, and soon it spread its broad leaves over Jonah's head, shading him from the sun. This eased his discomfort, and Jonah was very grateful for the plant.

But God also arranged for a worm! The next morning at dawn the worm ate through the stem of the plant so that it withered away. (Jonah 4:6–7)

THERE HAVE BEEN some who have speculated about what kind of plant (as in plant genus or species) the Lord made to grow at Jonah's shelter. I won't go into that. That means nothing to me. But the narrative lets us know it grew remarkably fast for even a very fast-growing vine (Jonah 4:10). Its sudden arrival demonstrates only the Lord could have caused it to grow.

To me, I simply see this as yet one more miracle God performed in the process of dealing with both Nineveh and Jonah.

Many people who lack faith in both the Bible and the God of miracles will of course have a problem accepting this part of the story like they have trouble believing the account of

Jonah's experience with the fish. But since God is the creator of all things, He could have easily caused the plant to grow at a miraculous pace.

Just as the Creator could have prepared a one-of-a-kind fish to swallow and care for Jonah for three days, He could have just as easily caused a one-of-a-kind vine to grow and cover whatever crude shelter Jonah built for himself.

The vine gave Jonah more relief from the heat of the sun, and all the time it shaded his head, he was thankful for it. In fact, he was *very grateful.* Surely he knew it could have been no coincidence that the vine grew where it did. And perhaps to Jonah, the combination of the vine's quick growth and the shade it suddenly provided was an indication to him that God had not forgotten about him or ceased to care about his well-being.

Of course that was more true than Jonah realized!

Perhaps Jonah felt encouraged for a time. Maybe his attitude even improved some after knowing that God cared enough to provide shade for him while he waited for the Lord's final response to the Assyrians' fast of repentance. But if his attitude improved, that improvement didn't last long; for once again he discovered God was still coordinating events to deal with him.

God was intentionally still dealing with Jonah's attitudes.

In a harsh, hot environment, a plant can wither rapidly without the work of osmosis supplying a continuous flow of nutrients and moisture through the plant's capillaries. And the worm God provided for the task of destroying the shady covering on Jonah's shelter worked quickly on the plant's main stem.

The Lord brought along a very hungry worm; the worm began chewing insatiably; and soon the plant's leaves wilted.

It's amazing how much damage a single worm can do, especially one arranged by God to be a guest at a preacher's pity party.

Jonah had to have started getting concerned when he saw the leaves beginning to droop. Perhaps he looked down at the base of the plant and saw the worm that had attacked his shade-giver. Perhaps he reacted as anyone likely would and killed the worm. But if so, by that time it was too late to save the plant.

God had a message to send to Jonah, and His resources and creativity to do it were unlimited then, just like they still are today. It's clear Jonah had a serious problem, and the Lord was determined the cause of Jonah's problem would not be ignored in any way.

Undoubtedly, God was determined to continue doing whatever He had to do to get through to Jonah—even if He had to demonstrate His control and will by doing yet again something we might experience in the flesh as a "bad thing."

Again, since the Lord saw to it that Jonah's story was placed in the Holy Scriptures, He intends for us to learn from Jonah's experience. God cared enough for Jonah—and if needed, He cares enough for us—to send a storm. He cares enough to prepare a fish for only one purpose. He cares enough for us to cause a miracle-plant to grow to provide us shade for our comfort.

And if necessary—in order for us to receive the message that He so wants us to receive—God cares enough to send a worm to destroy the very plant He first caused to grow.

CHAPTER 13

GOD CARES ENOUGH FOR ONE

And as the sun grew hot, God arranged for a scorching east wind to blow on Jonah. The sun beat down on his head until he grew faint and wished to die. "Death is certainly better than living like this!" he exclaimed.

Then God said to Jonah, "Is it right for you to be angry because the plant died?"

"Yes," Jonah retorted, "even angry enough to die!"

(Jonah 4:8–9)

THE PLANT WILTED quickly and no longer supplied the shade that Jonah had been so happy about receiving. The sun rose high in the sky, and the higher it got, the hotter it got. Then God arranged for *a scorching east wind* to blow.

If that was anything like what I've experienced in desert areas during my lifetime—in areas like Needles, California—it felt like a blast furnace. The sky was undoubtedly clear, and the sun eventually beat down on Jonah's head with such vehement force that he became faint.

As the heat robbed Jonah of his strength, his general attitude about life faded along with his feeling of well-being. His outlook declined more and more until once again he despaired of life. And accompanying his despair was another release of his anger.

God once again approached Jonah about his anger, and this time he responded to the Lord with the claim that he had every right to be angry. Jonah let God know he believed his anger was entirely justified, and he evidently was so convinced of it that he was ready to die to prove it.

Earlier, he wanted to die because he was upset and embarrassed by having to proclaim judgment on the Ninevites just to see them fast and pray. Now in the narrative, he wanted to die because the plant that gave him shade had wilted.

Things were just not going Jonah's way.

Jonah was thankful for the plant God provided. And he surely believed the Lord provided him the shade of the plant because He cared for him. But any good feelings about God causing the plant to grow were gone. Things once again turned sour for Jonah, and he saw nothing good to be had.

I believe Jonah was consumed by two overarching feelings. First, he was obsessed by God's injustice as he considered the likelihood of the Lord changing His mind about punishing the Assyrians. Second, he was gripped by anger over what he felt was God's mistreatment of him. As far as concerning Jonah's attitudes and outlook on life at the time, there was no fairness to be found anywhere.

He had not wanted to do what he eventually, begrudgingly did because of the pressure God brought against him. Of course Jonah knew he was in the wrong back then. It was wrong for him to disobey God, but he must have felt it was equally wrong for God to do what He was doing. And Jonah became so angry and frustrated over everything that he no longer wanted to deal with any of it.

He came to the place where he once again complained, and he exclaimed he would be better off dead than alive.

He wanted to end it all—again.

To Jonah, life was *so-seriously-not* going his way that he wanted to give up. He was even ready to give up his vigil to see God's final response to the Ninevites. Nothing mattered any more.

He was ready to lay down his ministry and die. He was ready to give up all hope and any future enjoyment he could ever find in life and service to His Lord. He felt like he had reached the end of the road, and he apparently saw no reason for putting any more effort into bettering his own circumstances.

Perhaps we should pause for a moment to delve a little deeper into what Jonah's feelings about his own life might have been like at the time. And as I considered that myself, the thing that came to me was the fact it really can be a hard thing for anyone who is truly tender in his or her relationship with God to handle personal failure.

Of course I'm not so sure Jonah's heart was very tender, but he sure had to handle some serious personal failure.

It shouldn't be lost on us that Jonah had known the satisfaction of serving God through efforts in which he was willingly engaged. Jonah had already been used by the Lord, and I assume he responded obediently to God's call in the past without hesitation. But since he was called to go to Nineveh—since Jonah attempted to run from God—his relationship with the Lord was more than simply fraying. In fact, it was coming apart at the seams.

Jonah had already suffered because of his bad decisions. And he likely realized his relationship with the Lord was continuing to deteriorate as his spiritual vitality went into further decline.

Long before the plant grew, Jonah was already having to handle his own failure and lack of agreement between him and God. And his own poor attitude and feelings of injustice were highlighted even more by the plant growing, providing for his need for only a short time, and then dying.

I can imagine Jonah thinking, "I didn't ask for the plant to grow! What are you trying to do to me Lord? Why manipulate my emotions like this? Why give me something good just to take it away?"

Jonah was a man dealing with anger and frustration. He undoubtedly felt God was being unfair; but he also had to have been extremely disappointed with himself. He knew he was at odds with God. He knew the Lord was dealing with him. He knew God had the right to order his life.

Ultimately, Jonah also had to know that if there was any disagreement between him and God, the Lord's rights and resolve would always prevail over his own. But even acknowledging and accepting the truth of all that was not enough to fix Jonah's personal problems!

God was dealing with an angry man; and clearly, He was dealing with the angry man *in intentional steps.* Step by step, God deliberately moved methodically to teach Jonah what He wanted to get through to him. Jonah's anger over the actions of both God and man—including, I believe, his feelings about his own actions—drove him into a pit of depression. The angry, demoralized preacher was not a good student.

But just as God's overarching interest in the Assyrians was to save and not destroy the people of Nineveh, His solution and goal in dealing with Jonah was not for a disobedient servant to be discarded but for him to learn and once again flourish in His service.

God's grace and mercy were not just displayed in His willingness to forgive the Ninevites; they were displayed in the Lord's ordered attempts to reach Jonah and meet *his* need. God's intentions and the lengths He will go to in order to salvage troubled lives—to salvage even one single life—become clear through the Lord's persistent pursuit of Jonah's heart.

God was indeed persistent and not willing to give up on Jonah. He was resolute in teaching him. And in all He was doing, the Lord was reinforcing to him in multiple ways that God's solutions for problems are redemptive in nature and not destructive. Jonah knew that, of course, but he had yet to come to the place where he was ready to apply that truth to either the Assyrians or himself.

God and Jonah were not in agreement about some important things. Jonah wanted the Ninevites to face God's judgment.

God wanted them to repent. Jonah wanted to die, but the Lord wanted him to not only live but also learn!

God's abilities are boundless. He can do more with one initiative than all of the plans we can draw up in a lifetime. And He can multitask in ways beyond our understanding. All through the story in the book of Jonah, God was taking care of many things through His actions.

When the Creator sent the storm to deal with Jonah, He also—at the same time—revealed the reality of His existence and involvement in the world to a ship's captain and crew. While He worked in the hearts of the king and each person in the great city of Nineveh concurrently, He was also beginning to bring to a head the problems in Jonah's heart.

The Assyrians benefitted from what God was doing. The ship's crew benefitted from what He was doing. I believe Jonah eventually benefitted from what He was doing (I address that later). And by learning from all of it even today, we are benefitting from it as well.

Something important that we can glean from the book of Jonah should be becomming clear to us by now. While God was doing so many things, while God was dealing with the Assyrians, while God was dealing with issues involving masses of people and indeed nations, He was simultaneously dealing with one solitary man—Jonah.

The Lord is moved by the needs of the multitudes, but He is also moved by the needs of each individual person—including me, including you, including each single member of your family, including each one living in your neighborhood, and we could go on and on.

Through the book of Jonah, God clearly demonstrates that while He cares for all the people who make up a nation, God also cares enough for one.

CHAPTER 14

GOD CARES ENOUGH FOR CHILDREN

But the LORD *said, "You have had pity on the plant for which you have not labored, nor made it grow, which came up in a night and perished in a night. And should I not pity Nineveh, that great city, in which are more than one hundred and twenty thousand persons who cannot discern between their right hand and their left . . . ?* (Jonah 4:10–11 NKJV)

WHEN GOD ASKED Jonah the first time if he had a right to be angry, we don't read that he answered Him. We read only that Jonah went outside the city to wait to see what God's final decision would be about Nineveh. But after the plant died, when God questioned his anger a second time, he answered the Lord. And following that answer, God showed His willingness (and desire) to have a broader discussion with him.

I imagine Jonah didn't want to have the conversation, but God was intent on it. It's common for people—yes, even preachers and other leaders—to have a tendency to avoid dealing with their personal issues. We're often content to avoid and ignore problems as much as possible. But God wants to deal with all of our problems. He wants to fix them, and He's patient and methodical in doing it.

So God confronted Jonah's attitude again after He caused the vine to grow and then sent the worm to kill the vine and take away his shade. The Lord had a higher purpose for that short-lived plant. Certainly, He cared for Jonah, who was suffering in the sun; but the Lord's care for him went much deeper than caring for his comfort or physical well-being.

God's main concern for Jonah was for the prophet who lacked both love and grace for others *to get his act together.* As we might say in a more casual way, Jonah needed his head *screwed on straight.*

Somewhere along the road in his life and ministry, he had gone off track when it came to understanding his mission and its purpose. And Jonah no longer had—if he ever really did have—a full understanding of and appreciation for God's true nature and intention for the world.

Jonah just wanted to die. Perhaps he thought that would be the ultimate way to avoid dealing with his own spiritual problems. Or he may have thought that was the best way to evade his responsibility to bring the Lord's solutions to others. But God would not let Jonah pass into eternity without doing everything He could to salvage his ministry and redeem him from a miserable end.

The Lord used this last event recorded in the book of Jonah to bring about yet another opportunity to deal with him.

In dealing with Jonah about the plant, God was basically confronting his spiritual value system. And incidental to the questions He asked him, there were actually many questions about his sense of values that Jonah needed to confront in his mind. Although those questions were not written down for us to read, they had to have entered his mind as the Lord made His points.

When God questioned him about his concern, surely one question Jonah had to pose and answer for himself was, **"What do I really care about?"**

The Lord confronted Jonah with his concern for the vine. He made sure that Jonah understood he had nothing to do with making that vine grow, and he also had nothing to do with its demise. To me, lesson one from that particular illustration was that God is the one who ultimately chooses the destiny of all life under His authority (which of course is everything).

Jonah certainly had the power in his hand to uproot the plant if he wanted to, but he could not make it grow. And the preeminence of God's position in Creation is further illustrated to us by the fact that even if Jonah wanted the plant to live and did everything he could to ensure that the plant would continue to grow, God had the right and the power to decide to send a worm to destroy it against Jonah's will.

Here is something important Jonah needed to understand (and so do we):

Just as Jonah was not responsible for choosing whether to give that plant life or take it away, he was also terribly confused if he harbored any feeling that his opinions on whom should be judged—or who should live or die in Nineveh—held any sway with the Lord.

God, alone, is the world's judge, and He alone will decide when His mercy held out to either a nation or any single individual has come to an end. That decision was not up to the prophet Jonah—**and it's not up to us today!**

Jonah's views about his own place in the world, and I believe his own feelings of importance, were definitely underlying his issue with the plant. You see, truth be told, it wasn't really his concern for the plant that set him off as it wilted away; it was his feeling about how the death of the plant *affected him.* It was actually his own disgust over losing that precious shade—the discomfort it caused *him*—that angered him and drove him to express his despair.

As we examine all that's recorded in the book of Jonah, it should not be lost on any of us by now that Jonah's concern about how things affected him was lingering somewhere around the core of all his troubles. And of course it only made matters worse to know that God was implicated in everything that disappointed and frustrated him!

Once again Jonah had an excuse for allowing himself and his reaction to be motivated by a grudging sense of injustice in every sense of the word. He was angry with God. Yes, I believe he was angry with himself. And he was without doubt angry with life in general.

Surely Jonah knew if he lived he would ultimately need to face head-on his feelings of injustice. And it seems clear that he simply couldn't seem to conquer his own desire to determine what merited either justice or grace.

Only by overcoming that—only by being able to prioritize God's interests in pursuing, salvaging, and rehabilitating lives over his own self-interests—would Jonah be able to accept the decision of the Judge of the Universe and receive the personal miracle, the change, that the Lord wanted to bring about in his life.

Becoming self-absorbed and resistant to accepting God's leadership will carry any of the Lord's followers into spiritual confusion. And spiritual confusion in our lives will always cause us great difficulty. Left unaddressed, it can even lead to our destruction.

God didn't want Jonah's ministry and life to come to a disastrous end like that. He was not going to allow Jonah to die without doing everything He could to deliver him from his spiritual death spiral.

After Jonah voiced the final pronouncement of his frustration that's recorded in his story, the Lord replied with the words that may have been the very ones to start shifting his understanding (assuming that happened). God drew Jonah's attention away from the plant he was getting all worked up about losing to focus on 120,000 innocent lives who would be lost if He destroyed the city of Nineveh.

The *New Living Translation* (the default version I used for this book) speaks of the 120,000 as "people living in spiritual darkness." Most other versions, though, follow the classic wording of Scripture found in the *King James Version.* And I used the *New King James Version* to introduce this chapter.

The popular understanding that has appeared in many Bible commentaries produced by reputable theologians and the teachings of Bible scholars for centuries is that the 120,000 persons who *cannot discern between their right hand and their left* refer to children who have not yet reached the age of accountability for their sins.

There are those, however, who point out problems with that number referring to children. At issue—what they point out—is that if there were 120,000 children that young in Nineveh, the city, they say, would have had to support a population of over 600,000 people. And according to them, studies they call out estimate the total population of Nineveh was no more than around 175,000.

Perhaps the translators and editors of the *New Living Translation,* which is one of the more recent translations of Scripture, let those arguments affect the wording they chose. I personally can't say. And I also won't say much more about the disparity. I'll simply say there are others who contend Nineveh supported a population of possibly up to or over one million Assyrian citizens. Based on their views, it's definitely not out of the question that 120,000 young children lived in Nineveh in Jonah's day.

Bottom line, I begin my study of the Bible by believing what it says and by discounting the views of its critics. God knew what he was talking about when it comes to the "120,000" number. So I begin by choosing to believe what He said just as it is recorded in the book of Jonah. If you believe the Bible is authoritative and inspired by God, the accuracy of the number itself is not open to question.

Then as for that number being applied to the population of young children in Nineveh, that is entirely sensible based on the wording of the large majority of Bible versions and a multitude of dependable sources who have examined the Hebrew language and the oldest manuscripts. But from a merely subjective standpoint, it also just makes more sense.

I used the NLT for the default Bible version in this book because of its readability, but I agree with and choose to go with the traditional view of the number accurately stated as referring to children. And by the way, even the note provided by the translators of the NLT for Jonah 4:11 reads; "Hebrew[:] *people who don't know their right hand from their left."*

So then, the question for Jonah to internalize was, "What do I care more about—the 120,000 innocent children of Nineveh who will die if God moves in judgment, or the plant that provided shade over my miserable head?"

God was addressing with Jonah the topic of priorities. What matters more, a plant or 120,000 innocents? And of course, that relates directly to problems with misplaced priorities Jonah had embedded in his heart and mind about several things.

With the death of a plant, the Lord was teaching Jonah that when it comes to what God values—and what Jonah (and we) should also value—God cares enough for children.

CHAPTER 15

GOD CARES ENOUGH FOR THE ANIMALS

> *And should I not pity Nineveh, that great city, in which are more than one hundred and twenty thousand persons who cannot discern between their right hand and their left—and much livestock?* (Jonah 4:11 NKJV)

GOD'S CONCERN FOR the welfare of the Assyrians' livestock may seem a bit trite in comparison to God's concern for the children of Nineveh, but the Lord clearly called them out to Jonah at the same time, so we should take special notice of it. God was asking Jonah to consider not only His judgment's toll on all the people in Nineveh, but also the livestock they owned.

One would think we should not need to be all that concerned about the Assyrians' livestock. After all, the animals were kept only for their benefit. If the Ninevites were destroyed, they certainly would have no further need of them.

The Ninevites used animals for transportation and to plow their fields. The livestock provided the Assyrians food for their bellies, milk for their children, material for clothing, and leather-goods that were used for multiple purposes. They actually served no higher purpose when it came to meeting the needs of the population of Nineveh.

As far as we humans are concerned—at least those of us who eat meat, who don't believe in reincarnation, and who don't view animal rights as equal to human rights—there really is no intrinsic, higher purpose for domesticated animals than their responsibility to meet our needs. And since Creation, it has been our right to maintain them for our profit.

Most of us no longer depend on animals for transportation and farming. We have cars, trucks, and tractors for those. But we still keep animals either for meeting our physical needs or for our enjoyment.

We eat domesticated animals for the preservation of our lives and also hunt wild animals for food. And as for the other animals we don't eat, they're also there for our enjoyment or benefit as they perform their natural functions in the world.

In the Creation Story, we read:

Then God said, "Let us make human beings in our image, to be like us. They will reign over the fish in the sea, the birds in the sky, the livestock, all the wild animals on the earth, and the small animals that scurry along the ground."

So God created human beings in his own image.
In the image of God he created them;
male and female he created them.

Then God blessed them and said, "Be fruitful and multiply. Fill the earth and govern it. Reign over the fish in the sea, the birds

in the sky, and all the animals that scurry along the ground."
(Genesis 1:26–28)

We also read later in Genesis chapter nine the confirmation to Noah that God gave us animals for meat—to eat—as nourishment to sustain our lives.

Then God blessed Noah and his sons and told them, "Be fruitful and multiply. Fill the earth. All the animals of the earth, all the birds of the sky, all the small animals that scurry along the ground, and all the fish in the sea will look on you with fear and terror. I have placed them in your power. I have given them to you for food, just as I have given you grain and vegetables.
(Genesis 9:1–3)

But even before that, there is evidence in the Bible that animals—mankind's livestock—were a source of nourishment or otherwise served the needs of mankind. It was Adam's son, Abel, who was a shepherd (Genesis 4:2) and pleased God by offering to Him the first sacrifice of a lamb to be recorded in the Bible (Genesis 4:4).

Historically, after the blood of sacrifices was presented to God, the animals sacrificed were usually eaten unless they were presented to God as a burnt offering. But even if the lamb that Abel sacrificed to the Lord was a burnt offering, Abel was a "shepherd," and shepherds have always raised sheep for wool, hide for clothing, and meat.

But that wasn't even the first time an animal was killed for the good of human beings. The Creator himself killed animals and made clothing out of animal skins for Adam and Eve after they sinned (Genesis 3:21).

God created the world and all that is within it as He saw fit. And as part of His plan, He created it all for us to inhabit and to sustain us. He carefully built an environment meant to support our lives before creating the first man and woman. And when He finally had the world prepared in a way that pleased Him, the Lord created human beings, whom He then appointed to procreate, subdue the earth, and rule over all the creatures He made.

The earth and all that was placed in it were lovingly and carefully created and prepared for us. It is all ours to use for our sustenance, our benefit, and our enjoyment. Of course it goes without saying that we should indeed feel a level of responsibility to care for what God made us to rule over.

Along with *rights* come *responsibilities.*

Although God created the world for us to inhabit and meet our needs, we should note that everything—all that we can think of in nature that exists in the world today, and all life that has ever existed—was created by God according to *His* purpose, not ours. We did not decide or resolve to create the world. That was the Lord's doing.

Read what Paul said in his letter to the church in Colossae.

Christ is the visible image of the invisible God.
He existed before anything was created and is supreme over all creation,
for through him God created everything
in the heavenly realms and on earth.
He made the things we can see
and the things we can't see—

such as thrones, kingdoms, rulers, and authorities in the unseen world.

Everything was created through him and for him.

(Colossians 1:15–16)

Although God absolutely did spend five days building everything in the world to support what He created on the sixth day—us—the Scriptures declare that in the end, everything, including us, was made *through Him and* ***for Him***.

The Bible goes further in describing the Creator's relationship with His creation in other places. In the last book of the Bible, *Revelation,* the Apostle John described what he saw in his vision of heaven's throne room. He wrote about the twenty-four elders who worship around God's throne. Then he wrote about four living beings who continually extol the Lord's greatness day and night.

Whenever the living beings give glory and honor and thanks to the one sitting on the throne (the one who lives forever and ever), the twenty-four elders fall down and worship the one sitting on the throne (the one who lives forever and ever). And they lay their crowns before the throne and say,

"You are worthy, O Lord our God,
to receive glory and honor and power.
For you created all things,
and they exist because you created what you pleased."

(Revelation 4:9–11)

In the King James Version of *Revelation,* verse eleven reads,

Thou art worthy, O Lord, to receive glory and honour and power: for thou hast created all things, and for thy ***pleasure*** *they are and were created* [emphasis mine].

All of creation exists for God's pleasure, for His intended purpose, and according to His will. But even beyond that, continuing with Paul's message to the Colossians, we read,

> *He existed before anything else, and he holds all creation together.* (Colossians 1:17)

God not only *created* all things, He's the one who holds everything together. Our creator is just as active today caring for His creation as He has ever been. He keeps it all working, and without His interest and activities to maintain order right now, the world would be in a lot more trouble than it already is.

Based on what's revealed in the Bible, it should go without saying that God has an interest in everything that goes on in the world. And He cares for all life that He created.

God's knowledge of the world's affairs and His continuing involvement in our lives is so absolutely detailed and complete that the Lord even knows how many hairs we have on our heads. And directly in context with the Creator's concern for the livestock in Nineveh, not even a sparrow can fall from the sky—die—without Him knowing about it.

> *What is the price of two sparrows—one copper coin? But not a single sparrow can fall to the ground without your Father knowing it. And the very hairs on your head are all numbered. So don't be afraid; you are more valuable to God than a whole flock of sparrows.* (Matthew 10:29–31)

After considering these things, then, it would be a ridiculous proposition for anyone who believes the Bible to think God would not care about the animals belonging to the Ninevites. The Lord's care and concern for life that He brought to Jonah's attention naturally extended beyond the importance of the Assyrian people to even the cattle they owned.

To this day, the magnitude of God's care continues to extend to not only our interests but also to the Creator's interest in the animals He saw fit to bring into being for His own purposes—regardless of whether or not we recognize or value them to the same extent.

And also take note of this: The Assyrians certainly understood the value of the animals God brought up for Jonah to consider. The Ninevites placed such a high level of importance on the animals they owned that they included them in their fast of repentance.

> *No one, not even the animals from your herds and flocks, may eat or drink anything at all. People and animals alike must wear garments of mourning...* (Jonah 3:7b–8)

Jonah knew of the king's inclusion of the animals in his proclamation. So it should have been no surprise to him that God brought the welfare of the livestock belonging to the Ninevites to his attention. It was entirely logical for the Lord to do so. Nothing was being overlooked by God for His use in bringing Jonah to his senses.

Prior to God's final conversation with him—that is, the final one recorded in Jonah's book—it's certain that Jonah thought nothing about the value of any collateral damage to anything owned by the people of Nineveh.

But God definitely cared. You see, God cares enough even for the animals.

CHAPTER 16

GOD CARES ENOUGH FOR THE WORLD

For this is how God loved the world: ***He gave****...*

(John 3:16 [emphasis mine])

JOHN 3:16 IS ONE OF, if not the most-memorized and quoted verses in all of Scripture. Of course the rest of the verse is, *"his one and only Son..."* But for now, I want to focus on the first part of the statement with the emphasis on the words *He gave.*

I pause again in our chronological examination of specific passages in the book of Jonah to take up this thought because of what I believe is its relevance to what the book of Jonah reveals. I find something clear but unstated in the account of Jonah's story, and I want to address it here:

> The extent of God's concern and care for all of Creation has always been and continues to be revealed through the remarkable ways in which its creator has demonstrated throughout history that ***He is a giver***. And clear evidence of that exists in the book of Jonah.

There was no greater act of giving than when God gave the world a Savior on the day Jesus was born in Bethlehem. And there was no greater gift Jesus could give us than to die for our sins some two thousand years ago. But our creator has also *given* to mankind an uncountable number of other things since the beginning of time—among them, life itself—and He continues His giving today.

God is Creation's benefactor, and the Lord's identity as a giver is an integral part of all His interactions with Creation. It reveals to us the eternal love of God,[21] And this simple fact is uniquely illustrated through God's care shown in the book of Jonah.

In chapter two I addressed God's involvement in some of what we humans understand to be "bad things." Undoubtedly, it was a bad thing when the storm hit that day. It was a bad thing for Jonah to be thrown into the sea. It was a bad thing for Jonah to be swallowed by a fish. It was a bad thing for a worm to kill the plant. It was a bad thing for that hot wind to blow.

And of course, to Jonah, it was a bad thing to be called to go to Nineveh.

But God was not just aware of those "bad things" and using them for His purpose; He intentionally caused them all! The book of Jonah makes it clear that the Lord was directly responsible for every one of those things. And God gave each of them to Jonah to correct his life's path.

While it may be a challenge for us to consume this thought, even all of those "bad things" can be seen as *gifts* from God. For without God giving those experiences to Jonah—and by

---

21 "The faithful love of the LORD never ends! . . ." (Lamentations 3:22).

extension to Nineveh—and without the Lord deliberately and decisively dealing with Jonah through those experiences (also a great gift in itself), it's likely that Jonah's heart and ministry could not have been salvaged.

Like parents who are willing to do the hard things required of them to demonstrate through acts of correction that they love their children more than the children realize, God is willing to do the same for us. It's a parent's gifts of correction that prepare a child for a successful life as an adult. And it's our heavenly Father's gifts of correction that prepare us for futures that God approves and blesses.

God has always shown himself to be the supreme giver. And we see the proof of His giving nature through all of the gifts of correction He gave to Jonah—gifts that ultimately relayed to him the Creator's love, patience, tolerance, persistence, faithfulness, compassion, . . . and the list could go on.

Jonah's heart was in bad shape, and if God had not demonstrated His love through such gifts to Jonah (again, all necessary for his correction), he no doubt would not have had an opportunity to enjoy the more desirable gifts of forgiveness and restoration that the Lord was wanting to give him.

All of the gifts God gives to mankind, whether given individually or corporately, prove how much He cares for us—for you and me. And what we find in the book of Jonah should help us understand and appreciate that literally any of God's gifts to us reveal in part the care He has for all of Creation. And with that in mind, it wouldn't hurt us to take another look at our key verse for this chapter.

When we quote or read John 3:16, it shouldn't surprise us that our minds are fixed on how the Creator's ultimate gift to us—God's one and only Son—is the Lord's gift to mankind. But we should enlarge our view. The Scripture doesn't say "For this is how God loved *mankind* . . ." The Scripture says "For this is how God loved **the world** . . ."

As recorded in the book of Revelation, God *gave* the apostle John a vision of the future, and in that future, he saw a time of great delusion in which all people will worship "the beast"—that is, all people except those whose names are written in *"the Book of Life that belongs to the Lamb who was slaughtered before the world was made"* (Revelation 13:8b).

Simply put, those words written by John inform us that the gift of Christ, along with every detail involved in bringing that gift to us, was already planned and prepared even before the beginning of the Lord's work in Creation.

God's gift of redemption had already been determined. In a sense it had already been procured and wrapped in a bow, already prepared to be given to us, long before Adam and Eve, the first sinners, were even made.

The plan of God—the act of God becoming man, and His act of allowing himself to become our final, all-sufficient sacrifice for sins—was already sealed and certified before Creation. All that remained was for God to reveal His plan on earth and for us to receive His gift.

All of the Creator's activities in dealing with the world over the ages, all of *His giving,* has continually pointed toward the fulfillment of His plans established long ago. And it's clear in

Scripture that those plans not only included the redemption of mankind but also the restoration of all of His creation to the state in which He always intended it to be.

I already established how Jonah's narrative was validated by Jesus during His ministry on earth. He used Jonah as the only sign He would *give* people to prove His authority—to basically prove to them that He was (and still is) their Messiah sent by God—while also pointing them to His own death and resurrection.

In dealing with skeptics—and put more strongly, His opposition—Jesus pointed them to what they would soon witness. But He was also pointing them to things that God long ago was revealing to mankind through Jonah's story.

While referring those who opposed Him to the book of Jonah to get them to recognize God's faithfulness in sending to them their Messiah, Jesus was also inviting them to read again about God's unmistakable interest in the continued existence of both the Assyrians and their animals.

And in that, Jesus was uniquely revealing to them God's care for the world—even in its corrupted state.

Taking together the message of Jonah and the mission of the Messiah, there is no missing how much God cares for the earth from the strongest and most influential down to the weakest and least of its inhabitants. ***This is how God loved the world!***

The truths we've discovered in Jonah's story about how much God cares for His creation have never been hidden from anyone who has been willing to acknowledge and accept them. But truths always have, and still do have, a way of going over the heads of those who don't pursue them.

The message of Jonah and the message of the cross are forever connected. Jesus made that connection. And it seems apparent to me that the connection goes beyond the three days Jonah spent in the belly of the fish and the three days Jesus spent in the grave. I see it extending to the revelation of God's gifts of mercy and grace for the world revealed to us through both messages.

To many the story of Jonah is foolishness. But the message of the cross has also been derided and considered foolish. For those who are willing to believe, though, both are gifts full of power and wisdom, and I see the message contained in one elevated by the other—with the message of the cross leading the way in honor.

> *The message of the cross is foolish to those who are headed for destruction! But we who are being saved know it is the very power of God. As the Scriptures say,*
>
> > *"I will destroy the wisdom of the wise*
> > *and discard the intelligence of the intelligent."*
>
> *So where does this leave the philosophers, the scholars, and the world's brilliant debaters? God has made the wisdom of this world look foolish. Since God in his wisdom saw to it that the world would never know him through human wisdom, he has used our foolish preaching to save those who believe. It is foolish to the Jews, **who ask for signs from heaven.** And it is foolish to the Greeks, **who seek human wisdom.** So when we preach that Christ was crucified, the Jews are offended and the Gentiles say it's all nonsense.*

> *But to those called by God to salvation, both Jews and Gentiles, Christ is the power of God and the wisdom of God. This foolish plan of God is wiser than the wisest of human plans, and God's weakness is stronger than the greatest of human strength.*
> (1 Corinthians 1:18–25 [emphasis mine])

God gave. He gave us the wisest of all plans and the greatest of all gifts (even though there are many who not only refuse but also criticize them). God *gave* to us the message of redemption—the message of just how far He was willing to go, and how far He went—to prove to us how much He cares. Then He *gave* His followers the Holy Spirit to instruct them, guide them, and empower them to reveal that message to the world.

God called and revealed himself to John, Peter, Paul, and yes, even Jonah, as well as countless others. He *gave* both them and the messages they carried to us as gifts—for our benefit. A result of their ministries was the revelation of the extent of His love and care. And He is still calling people today and *giving* them the mandate to continue the work of making it known.

To all who care to read the Bible or listen to those who teach and preach the truth contained within the Word of God, Scripture has always revealed to them God's existence as not only Creator but also the eternally-active *Giver* to the world He made.

The Lord, the Creator, doesn't want anyone to perish. So *He gave*. And although not everyone chooses to receive or acknowledge so many of His gifts to us, the Lord is still holding them out to us today, waiting for us to receive them in a clear demonstration to the world of His grace and mercy.

The Creator continually *gives* and supports life on earth! And Scripture proves that His care goes further than His care for mankind. Again, it extends to all of Creation. What is revealed in Jonah is consistent with God's plan to redeem not only sinners but also *the world* that contains and sustains them.

The total magnitude of God's care will be seen in the eventual restoration, or redemption if you will, of all things tainted by or affected by *the Fall*—all things affected by the entrance of disobedience and its curse into the world.

One day Jesus was teaching His disciples and speaking to them about the kingdom of heaven. He spoke of a future time when He would sit on the throne, and when His disciples would also sit on thrones as they participated in judging the twelve tribes of Israel.

> *Jesus replied, "I assure you that* ***when the world is made new*** *and the Son of Man sits upon his glorious throne, you who have been my followers will also sit on twelve thrones, judging the twelve tribes of Israel."* (Matthew 19:28 [emphasis mine])

The day is coming when God will forever reverse the effects of man's fall on Creation and *make the world new*. He is indeed going to judge the world; and according to Scriptures that speak of end-time events, His judgment is going to be terrible in its consequences. But after that judgment, He is going to renew all things.

Even the tree of life will be restored to us when God's plan is completed.[22] And the restoration of the tree of life is

---

22 One of the results of Adam's and Eve's sins was their banishment from the Garden of Eden and their restriction from partaking of the fruit of the Tree of Life (Genesis 3:22–24).

so significant that it's mentioned three times in the book of Revelation—from the beginning of Revelation to the end.

> *Anyone with ears to hear must listen to the Spirit and understand what he is saying to the churches. To everyone who is victorious I will give fruit from the tree of life in the paradise of God.* (Revelation 2:7)

> *Then the angel showed me a river with the water of life, clear as crystal, flowing from the throne of God and of the Lamb. It flowed down the center of the main street. On each side of the river grew a tree of life, bearing twelve crops of fruit with a fresh crop each month. The leaves were used for medicine to heal the nations.*

> *No longer will there be a curse upon anything. For the throne of God and of the Lamb will be there, and his servants will worship him.* (Revelation 22:1–3)

> *Blessed are those who wash their robes. They will be permitted to enter through the gates of the city and eat the fruit from the tree of life.* (Revelation 22:14)

The overarching message of God's activities on earth and the restoration of the entire world—all of Creation—is clear in Scripture. The Creator's plan for that restoration is set in stone. Consistent with the revelation of God's care in the book of Jonah, one day our incredibly active and *giving* creator will prove for all time that He cares enough for the entire world to carry out every piece of the plan He drew up so long ago.

I mentioned *Deism* in chapter one but spent little time talking about it. Now I'm ready to say more. There are many *Deists* in the world today (they are all around us)—even though most of them don't know that's actually what they are.

As I mentioned, Deists believe in God as Creator but also believe that once God created the world, He left it to fend for itself. Deists don't believe in the revealed truth of the Bible when it comes to God's continuing activity in the world and His complete plans for it.

They don't trust Him as their continuing, active giver of life. And they certainly cannot put their confidence in the One who revealed himself in the book of Jonah to be so personally active in the lives of not only nations but also individual people.

Deists don't place their hope for the future in the One God who is continually involved in His creation and who will one day usher in an eternal day when He rules over His creation in complete justice, order, and peace. And they don't acknowledge that it will take Him, and Him only, to bring it to pass.

Deism will not allow its spiritual captives to accept the truth of God's activity revealed in the story of Jonah and how it proves His concern for disobedient people and the world in which they live.

In the grip of Deism, people cannot accept that the Creator could possibly love His creation enough to give himself for it and be so involved in it to still be working on a daily basis to bring us all to a realization of His love and mercy.

Deism cannot tolerate the concept of only one Savior *given* to us by God—the One and only Savior capable of revealing to us how much God loves and cares for the world He made.

A Deist cannot accept the personal, ongoing, continual activity among us of the Holy Spirit, whose most important role is leading us to that Savior.

A person with a Deist view cannot see God as ever having been concerned about the livestock of the Ninevites, or *all the animals of the forest, or the cattle on a thousand hills* that God said belong to Him.

Deists can't accept that God spoke the truth in Asaph's Psalm—when the Lord said He knows *every bird on the mountains.*

O my people, listen as I speak.
Here are my charges against you, O Israel:
I am God, your God!
I have no complaint about your sacrifices
or the burnt offerings you constantly offer.
But I do not need the bulls from your barns
or the goats from your pens.
For all the animals of the forest are mine,
and I own the cattle on a thousand hills.
I know every bird on the mountains,
and all the animals of the field are mine.
(Psalm 50:7–11)

Deism cannot conceive of God being so close to His creation and caring so much for it. And Deism will never lead people to believe that God could be busy, even today, still proving through the story of Jonah and in multiple other ways just how much He really does care for them on a personal level.

Deists believe in God, but Deism will not save them.[23] Deism is wrong, and its adherents are being fooled and led away toward destruction by insidious, humanistic error.

Deism promotes a creator who gave us the world in the beginning but has no plans for it's future. And it does not encourage anyone to believe that creator will give them anything.

But the Creator revealed in and through the book of Jonah has not just given gifts to us in the past. He is still giving, giving, giving, and giving some more as He continues His work to save and redeem the world He loves.

God's actions included in the book of Jonah were not recorded for the benefit of the primary actors in the narrative. They lived it; they didn't need to read about it.

The only reason for the book of Jonah to have been written, and the only reason for that written record to have made it into the canon of Scripture, is that both the Lord and the writer of Jonah's story wanted us to read and learn from it. The same lessons God taught Jonah are still being taught today through the narrative in his book.

We can and should, therefore, view the book of Jonah as another of our Lord's great gifts to us. For as God's gift to us, the book of Jonah joins other portions of Scripture in yielding itself to being used by the Holy Spirit to reveal God's eternal plans, His concern for Creation, and the extent of the grace and mercy that He gives to all of us daily.

---

23 "You say you have faith, for you believe that there is one God. Good for you! Even the demons believe this, and they tremble in terror" (James 2:19).

Our divine benefactor—the Creator—showed His care for us by giving us the book of Jonah. And He cared enough for the world He made to give His one and only Son.

God cares just as much today. He made us in His image and *gave* to us a home among all the stars He set in space. And nothing in all of Creation is outside of His care.

Indeed, God cares enough for the World.

CHAPTER 17

GOD CARES ENOUGH; SHOULDN'T YOU?

> *Then the* L*ORD said, "You feel sorry about the plant, though you did nothing to put it there. It came quickly and died quickly. . . .* ***Shouldn't I feel sorry for such a great city?"***
>
> (Jonah 4:10–11 [emphasis mine])

AS WE MOVE toward concluding our study of the book of Jonah, we reach the crux of the matter, at least as far as what God was doing in the prophet's life. Jonah needed a wakeup call, and he certainly got one. His understanding needed to be both challenged and changed. And he was definitely challenged.

Jonah's heart was not where God intends a preacher's heart to be—where God intends anyone's heart to be. A preacher should not just speak for God; the preacher's heart should also be in agreement with the Lord's heart and intentions. And such should actually be said about every person—preacher or lay person—who believes in and follows Christ.

The nature of God's heart is redemptive. Jonah's was vindictive and unforgiving.

God was concerned about the future of the people of Nineveh, the city, and all life within it—even the animals. Jonah would have been happy for them to have had no future at all.

God determined that He had enough of Nineveh and its wickedness. He determined that the Assyrians would not be allowed to continue to exist with such power as they wielded in their condition. However, God also wanted the people of Nineveh to repent so He wouldn't need to destroy them. Jonah, though, wanted them dead ***even after*** they repented.

Jonah's feelings—the result of his views diverging from God's views—led to Jonah wanting to die in frustration. But God wouldn't let him die. God determined to do a work of redemption not only in the lives of the Assyrians in Nineveh but also in Jonah's life.

Even after Jonah prayed from the belly of the fish, even after God delivered him and let him live to get a second chance to carry out His will, his heart was not moved. In answering God's call and preaching to the Ninevites, Jonah did it only because of the pressure the Lord brought to bear against him. In his heart, Jonah was still an unwilling participant in the Lord's plan even after He showed him mercy.

God had every right to judge Jonah, just like He had the right to judge the Assyrians. The Lord had the right to do away with all of them—the Assyrians *and* Jonah—for being disobedient and having hard hearts. But He cared enough for everyone involved to go to great lengths to bring them to repentance, to teach them about His grace and mercy, to change their hearts, and to save them from judgment.

We know that while God is motivated first by love and a desire to redeem and restore, He is also, indeed, the God of Justice (the part Jonah liked best). The world's creator is its ultimate judge. He has the right to judge us, and He *will* judge the world. But only *He* can determine when it's time to stop sustaining us. Only He can decide when to withhold mercy and grace and take the world to task through acts of judgment.

From what we learn of Jonah, he seems to have struggled a great deal with the idea that he should leave it up to God to decide when to judge and when to provide mercy. Jonah's beliefs were certainly not in agreement with what Paul told the Romans when he quoted from Deuteronomy—which are words Jonah should have been familiar with.

> *Dear friends, never take revenge. Leave that to the righteous anger of God. For the Scriptures say,*
>
> *"I will take revenge;*
> *I will pay them back,"*
> *says the Lord.*
>
> (Romans 12:19)[24]

Putting it simply, Jonah still wanted the Assyrians paid back.

Adding to what I've already written about Jonah's feelings toward God, I'm sure Jonah viewed Him as perverting justice when it became clear to him from the actions of the Ninevites that God was going to forgive them.

I believe as seen from Jonah's perspective—based on his first complaint—if the Lord's actions were just, it would be seen in Him backing up the message of judgment that Jonah declared.

---

24 With Paul quoting from Deuteronomy 32:35.

And when it comes to God's response to that, it could have been appropriate for God to say to Jonah what He said to Job.

> *Then the* L*ORD answered Job from the whirlwind:*
>
> *Brace yourself like a man,*
> *because I have some questions for you,*
> *and you must answer them.*
>
> *"Will you discredit my justice*
> *and condemn me just to prove you are right?*
> (Job 40:6–8)

God will not tolerate sin forever. He will ultimately judge those who don't respond to His attempts to salvage their lives. But regardless of Jonah's views about God's justice—and regardless of our views—the righteousness of God's justice is perfect even when our earthly minds may not always understand it.

Scripture declares that God judges with justice and rules with fairness.

> *But the* L*ORD reigns forever,*
> *executing judgment from his throne.*
> *He will judge the world with justice*
> *and rule the nations with fairness.*
> (Psalm 9:7–8)

And the fairness of God's justice is always righteous and complete because it is attended by, and cannot be separated from, "*unfailing love and truth.*"

> *Powerful is your arm!*
> *Strong is your hand!*
> *Your right hand is lifted high in glorious strength.*

Righteousness and justice are the foundation of your throne.
Unfailing love and truth walk before you as attendants.
(Psalm 89:13–14)

The Ninevites were truly blessed to have God care for them so much that He made sure Jonah delivered to them the Lord's warning of impending judgment. And even though Jonah didn't feel blessed at the time, he too was blessed to have God care so much for him that He not only called him to the task of going to Nineveh but also gave him an impressive, divine revelation of His tough love through all of his experiences.

God wanted Jonah to be a preacher and prophet whose understanding and attitudes reflected His. So the Lord went to great lengths and poured out not buckets but barrels of mercy upon him in His efforts to straighten him out.

And to that end, the Lord asked Jonah one last question:

"Shouldn't I feel sorry?"

With God's final question to Jonah, He was challenging him to dig as deep into his heart as he could to assess his attitudes. The answer to that closing question in the book of Jonah should be easy and come quickly for anyone whose heart is close to emulating God's. But Jonah, the prophet of God, had allowed himself to succumb to a selfish, worldly view of things instead of making sure he maintained a godly perspective.

And God proved it to him.

The Lord finally used a plant and a worm to show Jonah that his values had become turned upside down somewhere along the line. If Jonah's thought process at one time reflected his Lord's mind and purpose, it no longer did. And God was forcing Jonah to realize that.

When God called Jonah to represent Him and carry His message to the Ninevites, the preacher began revealing himself as a man who placed more value on how things affected him than on how things affected others—and that extended even to how things affected God.

The rebellious preacher was more concerned about satisfying his own desires and wishes than doing the Lord's business. He was more concerned about his own personal gratification than preventing the suffering and eternal heartache of hundreds of thousands of people who would die without knowing God if the Lord's judgment were not turned from them.

After studying the book of Jonah and knowing what we now know, if we had been there with Jonah and been privy to God's conversation with him, it could have been natural for us to want to join the Lord in His efforts to change Jonah's mind and bring his heart in tune with God's.

"Jonah, get it together man!" we might have said as we scolded him. "Surely by now you know that God cares enough to save your enemies—even the very enemies of God!"

"By now you should understand that nothing in the world is outside the arms of God's care and concern."

"After all you've been through, Jonah—after all of God's efforts to salvage your life and ministry—surely you can let go of whatever is holding you back from acknowledging your own foolish thinking and allow God to change *you* just as He changed the Ninevites."

"What's your answer?"

"Shouldn't God feel sorry for the Ninevites?"

"Jonah! Surely you know now that *God cares enough*—even for them!"

"**Shouldn't you**?"

CONCLUSION

CLOSING THOUGHTS AND APPLICATION

WHEN READING THE book of Jonah, a person has the opportunity to be engaged by one of the most important and vivid stories in the Bible. The action in the narrative is striking and unique in Scripture, and so is the development of its theme.

In my opinion, no other short, single story in the Bible matches this one in its ability to reveal God's intent to get His will accomplished through whatever means is necessary. And it is unequaled when it comes to how God conveys in one brief narrative how much He truly cares and acts to secure the well-being and future of not only His people but also their enemies, His disobedient followers, and even the animals of the field—by extension, all of Creation.

The book of Jonah also reveals a great deal to us about how God's care relates to His patience. It shows us He is patient when dealing with those outside the faith. And it unwraps for us how longsuffering and determined the Creator is when dealing with those who are in His family of faith but who struggle to overcome personal failure, prejudice, or a disobedient nature—any one of which has the potential of undermining His purpose in their lives and destroying them.

Keeping in mind that the book of Jonah was first delivered to the Israelites, that's significant. For in Jonah's narrative, in addition to the sign of Jonah pointing to Christ's death, burial, and resurrection to prove His position and authority as Messiah and Redeemer, we see God revealing to them through Jonah's story His interest in the Gentile world—the Lord's clear intention and desire to also sustain the lives of Gentiles and bring them into His truth.

When Jesus spoke to the Pharisees and Sadducees, as recorded in Matthew 16:1–4, lying just below the surface of His message to them was the fact that Jesus, their Messiah, came to redeem the people of all nations—the dynamics of which even some in the first-century Church had problems dealing with.

For when Jesus pointed the spiritual leaders of Israel to the sign of Jonah to foretell His death and resurrection, the spiritual elite of the day could have learned a great deal by going back to the book of Jonah and studying it again. They could have received additional insight into God's broader intention to save and renew the entire world—all of Creation, of which the Jews were only a small part.

And by responding to Jesus' reference to Jonah and reading again the story of God's dealings with him, those Pharisees and Sadducees who in their hearts had already judged Jesus and wanted *Him* dead could have had an opportunity to learn something important. By studying Jonah's story again, they could have perhaps come to understand that Jonah certainly was not the only Hebrew spiritual leader being held captive by a skewed view of whose wellbeing was important to God.

As He walked among and taught the people, Jesus went to great lengths to reveal to them the Creator's heart. But like Jonah, the religious leaders among the Jews in Jesus' day had severe misconceptions when it came to understanding the truth and God's plans for the world.

As Jesus stood before them and revealed to them their own corrupt thoughts, the Holy Spirit was dealing directly with them just as He dealt directly with Jonah. God wanted to reinforce to them that His plan all along was to work through the children of Israel as the faith of Abraham was taken around the world and shared with all mankind.

The coming of Messiah, who arrived to move God's plan into its final phase, was a most critical piece of the plan. And Jesus wanted all of the spiritual leaders to understand what God was doing through His life. But all too many of them—the majority of them, in fact—would not allow God to change their minds.

They could not accept the magnitude of God's mercy and grace that He came to extend to them and others.

When called to minister to the house of Cornelius—a Roman army officer who lived in Caesarea—it was an unnatural thing for Peter or any other Jew to go into the home of a Gentile. And I'm sure it took every bit of both the vision God gave Peter and the direct words of the Holy Spirit spoken to him to convince him to enter Cornelius' house on that mission.

> *Meanwhile, as Peter was puzzling over the vision, the Holy Spirit said to him, "Three men have come looking for you. Get up, go downstairs, and go with them without hesitation. Don't worry, for I have sent them."* (Acts 10:19–20)

If Peter had not been in tune with the Lord, and if he had not been willing for the Holy Spirit to further reveal to him God's plan for the Church, he might have been tempted to respond to God's call in a way similar to how Jonah responded. And like us, Peter would not have had to physically run away to prove his disobedience to God. All he would have had to do was refuse to do what his nature and upbringing already made him inclined not to do.

But Peter obeyed the Lord and went.

Cornelius welcomed him into his house, and Peter shared with Cornelius that although it was against Jewish laws to enter a Gentile's home or associate with him, God had revealed to him he "*should no longer think of anyone as impure or unclean*" (v. 28). Then before Peter began speaking to all those gathered with them in the house, he asked Cornelius to share with him his experience that caused him to call for the disciple (v. 29).

Cornelius told Peter that when he was praying, "*a man in dazzling clothes was standing in front of* [him]" and told him to send messengers to Peter, who was then staying in Joppa—where interestingly, Jonah had hitched his ride on a ship bound for Tarshish. He was told to summon Peter from there to come to his home (vv. 30-32).

> *Then Peter replied, "I see very clearly that God shows no favoritism. In every nation he accepts those who fear him and do what is right.* (Acts 10:34–35)

Peter then shared the message of the Cross with those assembled there in the home of Cornelius, and before any altar call could be given, Peter witnessed the Holy Spirit descend upon those Gentiles, who, like Cornelius, may have feared the one true God but previously did not know Jesus as Savior.

Recognizing that the Lord proved He wanted to bring Gentiles into the Church by giving those in the house of Cornelius the same experience Peter and the others received on the day of Pentecost, Peter declared there was nothing to keep them from being baptized (vv. 47–48).

Peter accepted what God was doing, and the Holy Spirit was able to move Peter's heart and mind to not only do God's will but also allow God to change his thinking and attitude at the same time. That was not true of Jonah, though.

Even after God convinced Jonah to go to Nineveh, Jonah wanted nothing to do with any positive results that could come from any ministry to those Assyrian Gentiles. There was something persistent within Jonah that caused him to be unmoved by God's attempts to change his thinking.

But is there any reason for us to have any hope at all that God finally got through to Jonah? Can we have any hope that his heart was finally softened, and he eventually repented and came to accept and approve of the fairness, righteousness, and wisdom of God's ways?

At the very end of the book of Jonah when God asked His final question, and Jonah once again didn't answer (at least not as recorded in the written narrative), is there any evidence that Jonah sought forgiveness for being so wrong? Did the time come when his heart was changed? Did he come to love the world like God loves the world?

I, along with David L. Raines—who provided the foundation of this book through his preaching series on Jonah—came to believe that evidence exists. I agreed with Pastor Raines that Jonah probably, finally, ended up understanding things God's way. But that evidence is not clearly written for us to read, so this is opinion. You can decide for yourself. Either way, though, it doesn't change the central truths revealed to us in the book of Jonah.

As I noted, nothing is said in the New Testament about Jonah except for the words of Jesus recorded in the gospel of Matthew and the gospel of Luke.[25] And no one, including Jesus, said anything about Jonah's end.

The biblical record contains no revelation of what Jonah's final response was to the Lord's dealings with him. And just as the book of Jonah starts abruptly, it also ends abruptly with God's final question:

"Shouldn't I feel sorry for such a great city?"

Jonah's answer to the question is not given, but even though his response to God's question is not recorded, we know his spirit had to answer the Lord.

Without reading of a positive response from Jonah, we might feel we're left with no hope at all that Jonah's heart was changed. Our knowledge that Jonah was such a hard case could lead us to believe Jonah eventually ended up being a spiritual

---

25 Matthew 12:39-41, 16:4; Luke 11:29-32.

failure—joining others whose experiences with God (even as ministers) started well but ended poorly.

But we have something else to consider.

We need to realize again the importance of Jonah's story actually being recorded and placed in the Bible. For it is in the very recording of the narrative itself that David and I found our hope that both Jonah's relationship with God and his ministry were salvaged.

There are those who hold to a belief popular in some circles that the book of Jonah was developed by someone long removed from Jonah and published centuries after the years in which Jonah ministered—that Jonah had nothing to do with it. Keep in mind, though, that those who promote that idea (they definitely cannot prove their hypothesis) likely also don't believe Jonah's narrative is historical truth. They believe the book of Jonah is merely an allegory, or a story of fiction teaching a good moral.

David and I agreed they are wrong, and I continue to hold the view that Jonah's story is absolutely true. I also continue to believe there is no reason at all to think the narrative in the book of Jonah was told by anyone other than Jonah himself.

Who else would have related it to others? Who knew the events so well to have remembered the words of all the story's actors? Who could have known all the words spoken by Jonah as he cried out to God from the belly of the fish?

But further, and more importantly, when it comes to the idea that the book of Jonah was written many years after Jonah lived, why would another Hebrew writer even want to make up a story like Jonah's that contains a message about God caring so much for Gentiles and enemies of Israel?

And when it comes to how it found its way into the Hebrew Scriptures, why would spiritual leaders and theological experts in Judaism come to accept a fabricated story as part of their trusted canon of Scripture, especially when the story inevitably challenges those same spiritual leaders to address their own prejudices toward Gentiles? Why wasn't the book of Jonah eventually rejected from the final Hebrew canon of Scripture like the apocryphal books?

Certainly, Jonah could have told others about what happened after the fact, and then someone else could have written down his story; but what encourages us to believe that happened? Does it not make just as much sense that Jonah wrote it himself?

Do you have a difficult time believing the story of Jonah? Do you believe years of study and research must be dedicated toward digging out evidence of the authoring and truth of the book before you can believe its message is from God? If so, you're not alone. But it makes me ask, why must some people always look for ways to rule out simple answers that can merely be understood and accepted by faith and through a person's trust in the Bible?

Surely the simple answers are not *all* bad!

Why are the first inclinations of some people to disbelieve what the Bible says until it can be "proven"? And why in some circles must there always be a tendency for people to apply "higher criticism" and let liberal opinions or thought be exalted over faithful acceptance of what the Bible tells us?

But let's consider this further, because I have some more thoughts on the matter for you to think about.

If someone else had written the story of Jonah, making it merely someone's creative writing project, I believe many additional details would have been put in the story that Jonah did not include. Among those things would be more information about Jonah's background—and details like where Jonah was spit out on the shore, what his recovery was like, who else saw him, and perhaps compelling accounts of Jonah's interactions with the people of Nineveh.

I think more effort would have been put into developing a larger story full of juicy details to appeal to the imaginations and appetites of readers and their desire for satisfying curiosity.

As is, we're left with questions about things hidden from us by the author. And I believe Jonah is precisely the one who most likely wouldn't have been interested in relaying to others all of those details.

It likely meant nothing to Jonah for people to know where the fish spit him up on the shore. Why would that be important if His mind was on relating the extremely high importance of the things that happened—the things God had forced him to realize?

If he actually came to understand and accept what God was teaching him, and if he desired to reveal that to others, it probably wouldn't matter to him to relay to them how long it took for him to recover from the ordeal or what route he took to travel to Nineveh.

I believe if Jonah learned the lessons God was teaching him, his goal in recording his experiences would most likely be shown in a focus directed toward merely relating to the readers the things that revealed his past attitudes and how God dealt with them. And that's exactly what we have in the book of Jonah.

And as far as how his narrative ends, it seems to me much more likely that it was Jonah himself who made a conscious decision to end his story with God asking, "*Shouldn't I feel sorry?*" After all, Jonah was a preacher, and I believe he probably ended his narrative with those words to leave his readers with the same question God left with him. He wanted others to *think*—like he had to think.

Perhaps I'm wrong, but Jonah undoubtedly had to have come to the place of understanding the question's importance, and I can see why Jonah would want others to honestly consider the same question. If that question summarized God's dealings with him and finally brought Jonah to agree with God's heart, I think that would be the question he would also want to use to challenge others who could have attitudes similar to the ones he had.

But then there's one more thing that I consider. If Jonah didn't finally come around to agreeing with God, why in the world would he have wanted anyone to know about a story that paints him as a failure, embarrasses him as a prophet, and exalts the Assyrians before the eyes of Israel into a state of being forgiven by God? I think in that event, Jonah would not want to even *tell* anyone about what happened much less write it down.

Admittedly, these are mere ruminations of my mind about how the story could have ended for Jonah, but my beliefs that sprouted from these thoughts do not challenge or change any truth revealed in Scripture.

I believe Jonah finally came to accept what God was showing him. I believe Jonah's heart and mind were changed. And at least part of the evidence of that change is indicated in the fact that Jonah did not allow the story to go to the grave with him.

I contend Jonah wrote it down. And after writing it down he shared the story with others. I believe it was his intention to share the story because he wanted others to learn the same lessons he learned. Again, this is opinion. But I don't believe it's unrealistic, so I present it for you to consider.

By relating his story to others, Jonah was sharing with them the lessons and words he received from God. And when people first began hearing or reading his story, I believe he was alive and available to back it up.

From the beginning, I believe he convinced others of the truth of the story. And through the words written by him, those early readers were the first ones to be encouraged to understand the application of his experiences.

Eventually, even more people read his story as it was transcribed, and they too shared it. It was copied again and again. Over the years it was kept and shared with many. And as the Old Testament was assembled, it was so well-known and highly regarded that it was considered anointed by God and included in the historical records of the Jewish canon of Scripture.

Now I'm finished with giving you my opinions of how things ended for Jonah. It's important for us to finish our study of the book of Jonah with some dependable, biblical truth. And as we close, all who desire the truth should keep in mind the following three certainties.

(1) All Scripture, both the Old Testament and New Testament, are authoritative and were assembled under the guidance of the Holy Spirit (2 Peter 1:18–21), and they are profitable for our teaching, rebuking, correcting, and training in righteousness (2 Timothy 3:14–17).

(2) Jesus gave His approval to the Scriptures that existed during His life and ministry on earth, and those Scriptures are still available to us today in the Old Testament (Matthew 5:17–18).

(3) Jesus specifically singled out the book of Jonah and gave it His endorsement when He referred to Jonah's experience as both a sign of His death and resurrection (Matthew 12:39–42) and a sign He was sent by God (Luke 11:29–32).

For these reasons, when we read the book of Jonah, we should take its words to heart. And as we read, we should pay close attention to what God was doing then—and what He is still doing today through *The Message of Jonah.*

As we get to the end of Jonah's narrative, I encourage you to spend some quality time contemplating the final question God asked him. I've presented to you a reason to believe that Jonah finally answered God in the positive, and his life was changed. But taking into account the message—the harvest of truth—

contained within the book of Jonah, it's more important for us today to decide how *we ourselves* will answer the question.

Looking even beyond that, though, what about other questions God may pose to us personally? What if our thoughts, beliefs, and notions are challenged by God? Can we allow the Lord to change them?

Will our understanding be enlightened, and will our lives be changed through the Lord's efforts to bring *us* to our senses? How will we respond to His questions? Can we allow our creator to convince us of our errors when we're wrong?

If we believe the Lord isn't being fair because of what He allows us to experience in life, if we think He is not being just, or if we're challenged by the thought that embedded in His attempts to redeem the world is the fact that He cares about our enemies as much as He cares about us, can we accept we're wrong and allow Him to prove it?

Will God be able to change *our attitudes* with *His truth*? And if necessary, will He be able to convince us that something we've been taught or what we've believed all our lives doesn't align with the truth of God's Word?

Is it right for God to reveal how much He cares by calling upon His followers to emulate that same care? Is it right for Him to call people to leave their comfort and preconceived ideas behind them in order to do something for Him that goes against their inclinations?

Considering God's personal investment in not only each one of us but also the rest of Creation, should the magnitude of

His care compel Him to take extreme measures to redeem the world He made? Should God care that much?

Just as Jonah was left to answer God's question for himself, and since it seems to me that he wanted the readers of his narrative to ponder it too, I now leave with you the question I used to end the previous chapter with a minor modification.

It's the form of the question that Jonah himself had to consider as he internalized it. And we all would do well to pose the same question to ourselves.

"God cares enough! Shouldn't I?"

Put on your new nature, and be renewed as you learn to know your Creator and become like him. . . . Let the message about Christ, in all its richness, fill your lives. Teach and counsel each other with all the wisdom he gives. . . . And whatever you do or say, do it as a representative of the Lord Jesus, giving thanks through him to God the Father.

(Colossians 3:10-17)

NOTES

NOTES

NOTES

NOTES

NOTES

NOTES

The John Bunyan Collection

By L. Edward Hazelbaker

ISBN 978-1-61036-133-0

ISBN 978-0-88270-757-0

ISBN 978-1-61036-153-8

Add John Bunyan's three most popular books to your library today. Read them to appreciate the depth of Bunyan's understanding of Biblical truth and his dedication to Christian service. The language within each of these books written in the 17th century was carefully updated for today's readers by L. Edward Hazelbaker.

HER CALLING

Dr. Jamie Morgan

Her Calling is a mentor in a book. Dr. Jamie Morgan uses her decades of experience and insightful leadership to inspire women to fulfill their God-given destinies. All women called to ministry will be blessed by the practical guidance and wisdom shared by Jamie Morgan. Regardless of what God has called you to do in your ministry, this book will become one of your most valuable resources.

ISBN 978-1-61036-080-7

JAMIEMORGAN.COM